In the Silence of My Heart

Volumes 5,6,7

Kathleen McCarthy

CONTENTS

Volume 5: All Prophecies in the Year 2012
Volume 6: All Prophecies in the Year 2013
Volume 7: All Prophecies in the Year 2014

DECLARATION

Since the abolition of Canon 1399 and 2318 of the former Code of Canon Law by Paul VI in AAS58 (1966), publications about new apparitions, revelation, prophecies, miracles, etc. have been allowed to be distributed and read by the Faithful without the express permission of the Roman Catholic Church providing that they contain nothing which contravenes faith and morals. This means no Imprimatur is necessary. The Author wishes to manifest unconditional submission to the final and official judgment of the Magisterium of the Roman Catholic Church regarding the material contained herein.

A Nihil Obstat and Imprimatur attest that the work itself has not been found harmful to the faith and morals of the faithful. They are not endorsements of any claims of private revelations, apparitions, visions, prophecies, or miracles that may be found in the work.

FORWARD

We read in the Book of Ezekiel (Chapter 37:4-10):

"Then he said to me: Prophesy over these bones and say to them: Dry bones hear the word of the LORD! Thus says the Lord GOD to these bones: Listen! I will make breath enter you so you may come to life. I will put sinews on you, make flesh grow over you, cover you with skin, and put breath into you so you may come to life. Then you shall know that I am the LORD. I prophesied as I had been commanded. A sound started up as I was prophesying rattling like thunder. The bones came together, bone joining to bone. As I watched, sinews appeared on them, flesh grew over them, skin covered them on top, but there was no breath in them. Then he said to me: Prophesy to the breath, prophesy son of man and say to the breath: Thus says the Lord GOD: From the four winds come O breath and breathe into these slain that they may come to life. I prophesied as he commanded me and the breath entered them; they came to life and stood on their feet, a vast army."

How should the reader approach the messages contained in this book? If you approach it merely as a devotional that you read to gain strength for your day, you will surely be inspired but you will not get the full benefit this book has to offer you.

If you approach this with a sense of awe of how the Holy Spirit works through Kathleen McCarthy, you will receive a great example for your own relationship with the Holy Spirit but you will not get the full benefit this book has to offer you.

If you use these messages to be guided on doing the will of God the Father you will be closer to *"Thy will be done on Earth as it is in Heaven"*, but you will not get the full benefit this book has to offer you.

What must you do to get the full benefit this book has to offer you? Approach this book like dry bones eager to be animated by God's very life for these words have the power of prophesy! The power of prophesy is more than inspiration, instruction, or correction, though it is all of these things. The power of prophecy is animation! Becoming animated by God's life, truth and love.

Approaching this book as dry bones disposes us in humility to acknowledge our total dependency on God and that he is the source of our very life. Anything that we accomplish for Him must be animated by Him. This book is for everyone who is seeking to be animated by God whether you are a teen, a stay at home mom, a priest, a business owner, in a nursing home, etc. The messages in this book will help you to be animated by God Himself in whatever circumstances come your way.

Fr. Stephen P. DeLacy

INTRODUCTION

About Ten years ago, Thirty years after my own conversion, I was sitting in Adoration, where I felt The Lord speak to my heart saying: "Place My broken body in the arms of My Mother, there, The Holy Spirit will fill them with new life. I want one mystical body in My body." And so I did, ever since I have prayed for unity in the universal church. I have prayed that all would become one. One Holy, Catholic and Apostolic Church.

About Two years ago at prayer during Adoration, I was prompted by The Holy Spirit to deliver a message. A message with an urgency to "Ready My people", to speak about our Baptismal call and the new life of the Spirit of God within each baptized Christian which enables and empowers us to be authentic witnesses. Although I spoke about these things many times in the past Forty years of my apostolate, there was as I stated a sense of urgency, a new anointing to deliver this message. I was instructed to take this message wherever The Lord sent me to speak throughout the Church. I was told as I did so, many hearts would be set on fire and minds would be enlightened to the Truth and Sacramental Life of our one Holy, Catholic and Apostolic Church. Souls would come back to the Church through grace as The Word of The Lord was spoken. Many would be healed and delivered from darkness by Sacramental Grace and be infused with power to go and make disciples. "This is a time of a tremendous outpouring of The Holy Spirit on the Church and her faithful priests. A time of mercy and grace, flowing from My heart, through My priests to My people."

In July of 2009 while being at an Eileen George Retreat, Three individuals told Dennis Nolen to look me up and so he called me. After a brief conversation, relating to me how he was directed to me, he said he would come to the Corpus Christi Prayer Group in Upper Gwynedd, PA the next Thursday evening. After a month or so, Dennis asked me if he could record my prophecies. I said "No, this is where people share from their hearts." He continued, stating that of course he realized that and only wanted to record the messages I spoke and then would print them out for the group and distribute them each Thursday, as he felt they were meant for everyone to read and think about. Again, I said "No". Just that quickly, The Lord spoke to my heart and said only, "Yes". I immediately told Dennis, "You may record them". With puzzlement, he said but you just said "No?" Smiling I said, but The Lord just said "Yes."

So it began, Dennis started to record the prophetic utterances I believe The Lord was speaking in and through me. It will suffice only to say some began to share these words with others and many other lives were impacted and much fruit of The Spirit was being manifested in their lives including Dennis Nolen's own life.

Dennis and his lovely wife, Anne and beautiful daughter, Alex and I have become good friends, for this too I praise God.

Over Twenty-five years ago, when I finally responded to The Lord's call on me to begin to write, I received the words: "In the Silence of My Heart" as a title. I even had an artist draw it as I saw it in my mind's eye. When I wrote my first book, I was ever so surprised when I was led to title it: "What the World needs now."

I asked The Lord, what about "In the Silence of My Heart?" The response I received was, "You will know when and how to use it."

My Second book which I am in the midst of writing is to be called: "He is Alive", a book about Jesus' Eucharistic Presence in my own life.

When would I ever use "In the Silence of My Heart" I wondered?

Well, shortly after these particular prophecies began to be recorded, I knew with absolute certainty, the words were coming from within, "In the Silence of My Heart" as I listened to God's whispers.

Hence, as the recordings are compiled into one volume, I now know this is the time to use this title: "In the Silence of My Heart."

On December 19, 2009, I was led to call Dennis, telling him the first prophecy of September 10, 2009 to the last one of Advent, December 17, 2009, was to be signed "Volume I" and be put aside for now. I said I didn't know why, but had a sense there may be a "Volume II" and I would wait on The Lord for direction.

Kathleen McCarthy

Volume 5

Nihil Obstat
Rev. Msgr. Joseph G. Prior

Imprimatur
Archbishop Charles J. Chaput
Archiepiscopus Philadelphiensis
October 18, 2018

No portion of this book may be reproduced in any form without written permission from the Publisher:
Morning Star – New Dawn Ministries
P.O. Box 1446
Blue Bell, PA 19422
If unavailable in local bookstores, additional copies of this book may be purchased by writing to the Publisher at the above address.

Copyright, 2019 By Kathleen McCarthy
ALL RIGHTS RESERVED   ISBN 978-0-9641873-3-7

Artwork by Margaret M. Matt

PROPHECIES

1/5/12

There's so much darkness, darkness that just overshadows the earth. But in each of you is a light, my light, shining in you, and within each of you is the gift of my love ... the gift of my Spirit that I left with each and every one of you. When you were baptized into me you became a new creation. But time and time again you fall back into the old, the comfortable ... fall back into the depression, the anger, the darkness. The darkness would suffocate you. The darkness will bind you up. The darkness will bring self-pity, self-absorption. But you must turn to the light, the light of my love. My light is shining brightly. It'll rise up within you if you only call to me, and I will fan the flame that is flickering within you that the fire of my love might burn brightly within you, might well up within you washing away the debris, washing away the fear, washing away the doubts, the anger, the frustrations. My light shines brightly but too few see it. All they see is the darkness, overshadowing the earth at times. But I tell you when you allow me to live in you and shine through you, that light rises up within others, that fire is fanned by your faithfulness by the fire of my love within you.

Many storms have come and there will be a greater storm yet to come. And so I continue to prepare each and every one of you to remind you that you are called. You see, I call you each by name, each and every one of you. There is no one else, no one else that can take your place, no one else that can do the work that I've sent you to do. But yet you remain stifled, bound up, ineffective, and many of the circumstances that you find yourself in you'll get weary and tired and you feel like you can't go on ... that's because you're trying to do it yourself, trying to overcome the darkness, trying to bring your joy to well up within you. But have I not told you I have come that my joy might be complete in you? It will be my joy that will dispel your sadness, your confusion, your doubts and your fears, your anger, your frustrations. Do not allow the darkness to stifle my Spirit at work in you for my light wells up and rises up to dispel the darkness wherever my people allow me to move in them and through them.

    Each of you, do not be deceived, do not be deceived, for many will come and they will try to deceive you. But as you place your hope and your trust in me, I will give you wisdom and knowledge and grace and understanding to be able to move outside of the darkness and to dispel the darkness wherever I send you for my light is brighter. I am "the" light and I allow my light to shine in you. I have given you instructions before ... do not remain idle, do not remain confused, do not remain in darkness, for a time is coming when I will send you out to be a beacon shining brightly for others to come to me and find their peace, their grace, their strength and their courage and their hope in me. So let not your heart be troubled. Trust in me and trust in my ways that are not like your ways, they're far above your ways. Just live today and allow me to live in you to give you a peace that you have never quite experienced before, to give you a joy that is beyond anything that you could possibly imagine, to give you a hope that whatever has happened in your life regardless of your circumstances and situations that I will work it together for a greater good, for this you can trust, in this you can believe, for it is the truth that will set you free.

1/12/12

    You see, I want to give you so much more, so much more than you ever expect, so much more than you can even conceive that is possible. I am the giver of life and so all that I have I give to you. Many are not ready to receive it. Many refuse it. But you see, you have opened your heart and your mind and your spirit and so I fill you, often times to overflowing, so that you will always know and be aware of how good, how very good it is to walk with me and talk with me, to share your day with me and your life with me. You see, I'm along the journey anyway, and isn't it more comfortable when you talk to a friend when you're walking rather than walk the journey alone being filled with a lot of thoughts without clarity, a lot of questions without answers? So yes, I am with you always walking with you, living in you and through you. So talk to me. Share with me. Share your concerns, your fears, your anxieties, your doubts. I know them all anyway, you know? So I just give you an opportunity to allow you to have the freedom to speak. And then listen … take the time to listen. Listen to my

Spirit working in you and giving you answers, clarifying things that you're confused about.

I'm always about healing and reconciliation. I always want to heal and bind up wounds. I'm always about forgiving, and then I call you to forgive others as I have forgiven you. That's the part you forget ... forgive others as I have forgiven you. There's so much, so much that I want to give you but you wouldn't be able to absorb it, you wouldn't be able to comprehend it all at one time. So I call you to grow a little more perfectly into my likeness and image day in and day out, and to accomplish that, you have to listen. You have to listen to the promptings of my Spirit within you. You have to listen to my Holy word as it's proclaimed to you through the Liturgy. You have to ponder it and ask what does this word mean to me today and how can I apply it more fully and completely in my life? You see, you call to me and say "Speak Lord", but you really aren't listening, you're busy continuing to talk. So I ask you, when you hear my word proclaimed take the time to listen. Hear what I've proclaimed to you and then act upon it.

It is written that I will pour out my Spirit on the last days. I will pour out my Spirit, and sons and daughters of mine will prophesy. See, it's expected! Don't be so shocked when it happens that anyone would hear my voice and proclaim my word and share the good news of my Spirit living in them. My word is being proclaimed through my priests or my deacons, and through each one of you by your living and authentic witness to the truth. I've told you again that the old will dream dreams and yet dreams were such a part of me speaking to others guiding them and leading them, and today you wouldn't believe it if someone shared their dreams with you and said they felt like it was me guiding them and leading them. But again, do you listen? Do you take into your heart my prophetic word? Do you take into your heart my spoken word which is living and effective? Indeed, old men will dream dreams and young men will have visions. Do you believe that this still takes place today or do you think that the Spirit of the living God is so stifled that no one sees the visions, no one hears the message proclaimed through the prophetic utterance, or that no one understands or believes in dreams … the dreams that I place in your heart, in your mind, and in your spirit? So you see, an authentic witness believes all that I have said, listens to all that I say, and then puts into action all that I call you to do.

Do not be idle, it is indeed the devil's playground, but be busy in the things of God. Be about my work, about building my kingdom, and your heart will never be troubled.

1/26/12

My word is spirit and life so that when you hear my word, when my word takes root in you, it brings my life alive in you so that you can live your life to the full. My word is all powerful. I say it again, my word is all powerful. My word is above every other word. When my word goes forth it goes and does the work it was sent to do to accomplish my will, my way, in my timing. Often times you do not understand it. Often times you struggle against it. Often times you fear it and doubt it, but my word is spirit and life. My word is above every other word. And when I speak my word in authority, in power, in might, all things come together and work together for my will, not yours, not someone else's, but my will.

And you have a choice, you have a choice to believe the word that is written in the papers, the word that is spoken to you through others, the word who tells you lies, the word that is often spoken in confusion and doubt, anxiety and fear, but my word you can trust. When I speak, I need no one else to confirm my word for I am the word, and when I speak, my word is brought into action through the power of my Spirit. So too it is with you. When you hear my word, when it drops into your heart, when you act on my word, my Spirit wells up within you, dispels the darkness, the anxieties and the fears, dispels confusion, it gives clarity of mind and spirit. My Spirit wells up within you and washes you clean, according to my word when it is proclaimed. So abide in my word, not the words that would frighten you, deceive you, not the words that would confuse you, not the words that would bring about fear, but search the scriptures for my word. Pray to the Holy Spirit so that the Holy Spirit will touch you in your mind and transform your mind into the truth that I am renewing you in mind, body and spirit.

Do not be deceived. Many will come to tell you lies, half-truths. You only need to ask the power of my Holy Spirit at work in you to reveal the truth to you, the truth of my word living in you. My word, my life, my Spirit I give to you through the Church. Mother Church gathers you, teaches you, feeds you and sends you forth. And in you, as you receive my word, it is through the power of the Holy Spirit that it'll be activated in you. And you have a choice to respond to my word and the authority of my word and the truth of my word and the power of my word or to trust in the word of mankind.

2/16/12

You are at the right time and the very place that I have chosen you to be for I will speak my word into your heart, into your mind, and into your spirit. You must cultivate it you see. To hear the word is one thing, to act on the word is another. I am raising up my people. My word is going out in power and might, and I call my people to stand firm ... stand firm in the face of adversity, persecution, trial and tribulation. Satan indeed is roaring like a lion trying to devour souls that are weak, trembling, those that are even standing in faith. But I tell you this, if you keep my word and allow my word to live in you then I will begin to move powerfully, the likes that you've never seen before.

I am calling my people to unite, to be aware of who they are: children of the most high God. I will never leave you orphaned nor leave you lacking. I myself place my hand over you. I will guide you and lead you out of harm's way. I will lead you in the paths where my peace and grace and strength will flow in you and out of you to others. You will be a "peace giver" in the midst of a storm. You will be one that carries the heart of Christ to those who feel unloved. There are so many, so many, and time is short. So I call you to use the gifts that I have given you. You see, my people will be amazed. They will be astonished when they see the power of my might working in and through my sons and daughters. But I would have them be astonished and amazed more so of the fact that you will bring them the gift of my heart, the gift of my mercy, the gift of my unconditional love, the gift of forgiveness, the gift of compassion. This is what the world needs and this is what the world needs now. Do not let anyone mistake kindness for weakness. Stand firm and be assured that I go before you. I not only prepare the way but I prepare my people. You are my warriors and I equipped you for the work. I tell you this day, let it be known that this day I say to each of you do not fear, I am with you. Do not be dismayed of the things that you will see and the things that you will hear for I am with you. All you need to do is trust in my love, take my word which is living and effective, and allow me to live in you and flow through you. I will do the work. I need you only to give me the opportunity to work in you and through you.

Many, many will cry out. Many will ask where is God? Many will fear and tremble, but you, you will know there is no need to. You will know that it is because of lack of faith, lack of hope, lack of trust that they cry out, that they wonder where there is and where there is not hope. They will cry out and wonder where is their God? But yet, they fail to recognize me in their everyday life, in their lives, in their homes, in their families, in their businesses, in the world. I tell you to take the weapon of my word that can do more than you could ever possibly imagine. This is what will astound people. This is what will amaze people. Then in the midst of darkness and turmoil you are at peace knowing that I am with you, knowing that I am God and I am working all this together for a greater good for my perfect will to be accomplished on this earth.

So again I say, let not your heart be troubled. Trust only in me. I will light the path before you and my word will be a lamp unto your feet so that you will not stumble and fall. Be at peace. Trust and do not doubt, and when I come I will take you with me to a place that I have prepared for you. But it will be in my time, in my way. I ask you again, do not look and have eyes but do not see and have ears but do not hear, listen to my word. Listen with your heart. See with the eyes of your heart and know that I am moving powerfully and quickly. Again I say, do not be dismayed, alarmed or afraid. I am with you. I will never leave you nor forsake you.

2/23/12

I've spoken to each of your hearts very specifically, and I call you on to this Lenten journey to grow. I stretch you because you open up your heart and your mind and your spirit to me. You give me an invitation to move in you and through you. But as the days of this Lenten journey go forth, will you continue to realize that you are accompanying me on this journey and I am accompanying you? I giving you grace, strength, food and nourishment for your soul, you giving me comfort and love, pure and simple. I want to touch each of your lives in such a way that I want to empower you and embolden you so that you might enable others to see me more clearly.

   I have left you my Spirit, the very soul of my mystical body, the Church. You see, you need not look anywhere else and yes, some of you do, but you need not look anywhere else. I have given you everything necessary in your one, holy, catholic and apostolic Church. I am present in the Eucharist. I have given you my priests who bring me present on the altar, every altar all over the world. And when this takes place I give you my life, my life I give to you as I feed you and nourish you with my own life. And it is in receiving my life in the Holy Eucharist, it is in receiving my life that you will be able to transform the world by transforming each heart that I bring you in contact with because it'll be me working in you and through you. You will have my life within you so that you can reach out with my love, you can speak with my voice, you can embrace with my arms, you can go and bring the good news to others with the feet that I will bless and anoint to carry my word. I have given you the gift of my Holy Spirit to accompany you on the way. You must stir up the gifts! You must remember daily who I am and who you are because of me. I have given you the sacramental life of the Church so that through the priest you can receive my forgiveness, my healing, my love and mercy through the sacrament of

Penance. So many look at this as old-fashioned, so many think there is no need, but if you have wisdom that is from above and you open your heart to that wisdom, the wisdom that when you ask for I give in a double portion, then you will continually go for the grace in the sacrament of Penance so that my life will continue to grow in you, that my life in you may touch others and transform their lives, that through you they might come to know me. Stir up the Spirit that I have given you from Baptism. I have empowered you to go forth and make a difference in the world. This is a gift and yet so many never give it a second thought. Not only have I gifted you with salvation, I have gifted you with the gift of my Holy Spirit working in you and through you so that you will come home to me as my son, as my daughter who have walked the journey and allowed me to walk and live and move in you and through you. So I tell you, you need not look anywhere else. I have given you the Church to teach you. I have given you the Church to guide you and lead you. She will not, I say this again, she will not be destroyed though many will come against her. It is through your hearts, your faithfulness, the power of my Spirit at work in you who believe, that will draw others back. The churches may seem empty at times, that is why you must go out into the world without being part of the world, that is why you must ponder the fact that because I am, you are in me and I am in you.

    Stir the gift of the Spirit. Stir it into flame. Allow the fire to burn brightly in you. I will not only cleanse you from the inside out, I will not only fill you with the fire that would purge you day in and day out from self, but I will fill you with the fire that will burn so brightly that it will warm the coldest of hearts, and the brightness of the fire of my love shining through you will indeed show others the way. Use your gifts that you have been given. Stir up the fire of my Spirit at work in you and decrease so that I will increase within you, and then go forth and be "Christ-givers". Go forth and be a light shining brightly in the darkness, a light that the darkness could never overcome. Remember who you are. Remember that I dwell in you and remember that I will empower you and embolden you to be a light in the darkness and a sign of hope to a people in despair.

3/1/12

I call you together to listen to my word and allow it to take root in your heart. I speak to you collectively, but I speak to you individually as well. Each one of you, every single one of you are mine. I paid the price for each and every one of you, and now I call you to stand in the gap, stand in the trenches. I call you to have a battle cry and your battle cry shall be: *"Christ crucified. Christ has risen from the dead, indeed, He has risen."* That's your battle cry. That's your power. That's your truth. That's my living word at work in you.

The time is urgent, urgent indeed. It is a time to stand in the gap for your children, for those who have not accepted me as their Lord, their Savior. Oh, they've heard the word. You've taught them about who I am, but now they have to figure out who they are. What is the purpose and meaning of their life? Am I here just for myself or am I here to change, to make a difference in the world? That is the thought of each one of them. You don't see it as that. You see them as doing their own thing, thinking only of themselves, their friends, but I tell you this is an urgent time. You must stand in the gap for them. Your battle cry again must be: *"Christ crucified. Christ has risen. He has risen indeed."* That is your battle cry.

Without the cross, without that cross in each of your lives there is no strength, there is no power. It is through the cross, through the suffering, through dying to self, through loving you so much that I was willing to end my life. Nobody took it from me. I was willing to offer my life back to the Father for you, for love of you. You think you love your children? It's a glimpse, a glimpse of the love that I have for each one of you. I seek, I seek you out. You can not run from me nor can your children, though they try, though they stumble, and though they fall. Do not forget from whence they came. Did you not stumble? Did you not fall? Did you not go down the wrong road on many occasions? Do not condemn those who do not know me whether it be your own children, people that you work with, people in your community, and the people that are in responsible positions. Do not condemn them. Pray for them.

What the world needs now is not a definition of my love. What the world needs now is a demonstration of my love ... a love that is willing to sacrifice, a love that is willing to give rather than take, a love that will stand in the gap for all those who have lost their way or have not known the way. Do you believe that I am? Do you really believe in the power of the cross? Do you really believe that through the power of the cross I was raised up for each and every one of you, not just for you, not just for your family, not just for those that you know, you love, and you care about ... also for all those that you hold in distain, all those that you feel are not worth praying for, sacrificing for. Those are the ones who need you the most, my children. Those are the ones I call you to stand in the gap for.

It is urgent and so the call goes out to fast and to pray and to stand firm. I will watch over you, protect you, guide you, and lead you. Trust, trust in my divine love. I have carved each of your names in the palms of my hands. I hold each of your hearts under the heart that was pierced for love of you. Know that I suffer for souls. One soul all heaven rejoices over. Will you stand in the gap? Will you be my voice? Will you bring the message of my love? Ponder these words. Ask yourself, how much are you willing to give for love of me? I can not be outdone in generosity. The more you give, the more grace I will give to you. I will fill you up with the abundance of my tender mercy and I will draw you even deeper into the mystery of my love.

Come to me if you are heavily burdened and allow me to assuage your wounds of your heart, of your mind, and of your spirit. I see all your hurts and all of your wounds. I see the scars of the battles you have fought and I tell you now you are precious in my sight. I will not leave you nor abandon you. You are mine and I have paid the price in full. Do not waste, I say it again, do not waste the gift of salvation but come to me for I am always here, always now. Every moment is "now" for me. Every moment is eternal. So come to me with all your burdens, all your hurts, and all your wounds and I assure you I will make you "wounded-healers."

3/8/12

Have I not told you, time and time again, have I not told you of my love, have I not told you of my mercy, my compassion? Have I not told each of you through the breaking of my word time and time again, the word proclaimed, that I can do more in you than you could ever possibly imagine? Why do you stifle me? Why do you feel that situations are hopeless or that I could not move in these circumstances that you struggle through? And so you do not come to me. You'd rather struggle through it. But you see, I do work in you and through you when you're aware of me working and even when you're not.
  I joined spirit and flesh together when I created you. Your soul is created in my likeness and image joined together with your flesh so that you will never be without my touch, so that you will never be alone, so that you will never be apart from me. I tell you this, you may dream dreams, you may dream dreams that are wonderful to behold, and your greatest vision, the greatest vision that you could think of, you could have hopes and desires of the greatest gifts and pleasures of life, but my people, nothing, nothing could compare with the gifts that I have given you, the gifts that you take for granted, the gifts

that I surround you with ... the sun and the moon and the stars, the beauty of creation, the climates, the people that I have brought into your life, the families that you have, the loved ones that you cherish. These are the gifts that I have given you, given from my heart to your heart, given freely. You did not pay, you did not earn them, because nothing, nothing could earn my love. I give it freely to you although it cost me everything to give you my Spirit, my Spirit which is at work in you purifying you and healing you, binding up your wounds, strengthening you in weakness. These are all pure gifts, gifts that you take for granted day in and day out. So many want to follow their dreams, chase after the desires of their hearts and yet they fail to recognize that I have given them the very gifts that will lead them into eternal life. All else is in vain. But you, each and every one of you, I have given you my Spirit to dwell in you ... my Spirit so that you would never ever be alone ... my Spirit that will sanctify you from the inside out ... my Spirit that will burn away everything within you that will stifle the power of the living God at work in your life. But I ask you to remain open. I ask you to come to me. All the gifts that I give you, each and every gift is free and yet these gifts so often you wish were not part of your life, especially sometimes when there are people in your life that rub you the wrong way, the people that you struggle with, the people that you argue with, the people that you don't like. Actually, they're the very people I send in your life to sanctify you ... to grow in forgiveness and love and mercy and grace. Those very ones, they're the ones that I sharpen you with. They're the ones that need your prayer, need your example of the Spirit of the living God in you for the fire of my love in you will indeed flow out of your heart and warm their hearts, melt their cold hearts. These are the gifts that you don't recognize. These are the gifts that you don't often want. These are the gifts, the many gifts, that I bring into your life moment to moment, day by day, and these are the very gifts, the very gifts that I died to give you because these are the gifts that will enable you to enter into the kingdom. Your life here is temporary. Don't be attached to the things that I have given you. Don't be attached to the things that you think you've earned on your own. In the blink of an eye they will all be gone. But my Spirit at work in you, sanctifying you, burning away all that would stifle my Spirit at work in you ... these are the gifts that are eternal. Trust in my love. Call upon my Spirit and know that I will never leave you nor forsake you and that I am with you always.

I call you especially again tonight to pray for your priests, for the greatest gift, the greatest gift that the world has ever known is the gift of my life ... my mind, my body, my Spirit that feeds you and nourishes you, strengthens you, enables you to become what you receive. This is the greatest gift. Never take it for granted, for the gates of hell will not prevail against it. But I tell you this tonight, your faith has been a gift, a magnificent gift. Hard times are coming, surely coming, and I am preparing you for those times. There will be times you will not be able to carry a Bible so I write my word in your heart. Listen and have ears to receive my word. Let my word sink within you. Go to the sacramental gifts that I have left you. I've left them because without my precious body and blood strengthening you, without the sacramental life of the Church, time and time again, healing you, forgiving you and sanctifying you, you would not make it home to me. So this is why I say pray for your priests. Pray for the gift of faithfulness. Pray for the gift of holy boldness, for without them the sacrifice would not take place ... the unbloody sacrifice would not take place. Pray for your priests daily.

And I say to you again, do not be afraid. I will take care of my own. But you look around and can not understand what will be taking place. Know this ... I am Lord over it all and I will work everything together for a greater good for my holy will to be accomplished. There is nothing to fear. Trust me and trust in my love for you. If I loved you enough to lay down my life for you, and I did lay it down freely, if I loved you that much, do you think for a moment that I would not take care of you and yours? Stand in the gap. Pray for those who are on their way to be lost. It is the fire of my love, my word, and the sacramental life of the Church that will flow out of you snatching them from eternal fire, for my love and my mercy is great and I would have none lost.

3/15/12

I am doing something new. I'm always about new life ... new life in the power of my Spirit, new life springing forth in the hearts of my people. I have heard your supplications. I have seen your tears. I have felt your pain. I've even seen your confusion and your doubts, but I say to you that I'm doing a new thing in your heart. I'm calling you deeper into the living water of my Spirit. I'm washing you, renewing you, reviving you. Oh, I have a mighty work for you to do, a work that you have not grasped nor even imagined. This is why I have called you here. I am preparing the way. My people seek healing. My people seek wholeness, and where there is brokenness, I want to bring new life.

Your fears and your anxieties about your children, your loved ones, reaches my ears like a fragrant incense. Oh, I know what it feels like to see your children wander off. I have watched many of my children wander … wandering, seeking. They do not know, have not yet fully grasped, the meaning of their purpose and my plan for their life. Again I say, I am doing something new, and the work I'm doing is in you and through you, that they will see in you new life, a new peace, a new grace, a new strength, and my love will well up within you and flow out of you. You will handle situations and circumstances with a strength and a power and a grace that you did not have before, and others will see and they will say, surely it is the Lord, truly it must be the Lord. They will begin to question. They will fight and be resistant, but I will have my way for I will give them new life. So let not your heart be troubled. Do not fear but continue to pray for your children. Many are on roads that will lead away from me. Nothing is more powerful than a praying heart of a mother, of a father, of a child for their parent. So I say to you, be assured, I am doing a new thing not only in your lives but in the lives of all those that I will bring into your contact. Where you were weak I will give you my strength. I will place a new song in your heart. And for all those who walk in darkness, all those that would try to slander or come against you, I tell you make no mistake, they will be exposed. My light will dispel the darkness.

In my one, holy, catholic and apostolic Church I am calling and gathering my people. I am raising up my people. I am uniting, through the power of my Holy Spirit being poured out, my people who have been separated, my people who have not found the fullness of truth, my people of other faiths. I am uniting my people through the power of my Holy Spirit. Make no mistake about it, it shall come to pass.

I ask you to stand firm. I ask that you would speak freely of what you have seen and what you have heard and the power of my Spirit that has touched your lives. It is this witness, it is this power, it is this healing grace that will unite my people. I have told you that the kingdom of darkness and the kingdom of light shall clash. But I tell you, when I shed my light, the darkness will disappear. Be at peace and be about the work of the kingdom. Be about spreading the good news. Do not keep it, do not keep it to yourselves, but spread it to everyone you know … more by how you live than what you say. But through your words others will listen and I will drop a word into their hearts. My people are in need of healing. It is in my one, holy, catholic and apostolic Church that they will find healing from grief to grace, from being lost to being found. I assure you, this will come to pass. I assure you, make no mistake about it, I am moving powerfully and I am doing a new thing and you will be my witnesses.

3/22/12

I want you to know, each of you, every single one of you, I speak to your heart. Even though you have ears to hear and your heart is open to receive my word, many will hear that are not present, and the word I speak to each of you now for it is always "now" with me. It is always "present", the present moment. It is always "now." I am outside of time and I'm outside of space. It is always "here" and "now." Here and now I want to bind up your wounds. Here and now I want to refresh you and restore you. Here and now I want to speak to your heart to give you new hope. Here and now I tell you, make no mistake about it, I am with you always, whether you're aware of my presence or not, I am with you.

And I can tell you how it delights my heart to see you smile when you think of me, how my heart rejoices when you recognize me in the moment. These are great moments of grace, but you would have a lot more of them if you recognized me in the present moment. Time and time again I wait to see if you know it's me who has blessed your day, who has worked so much into a small amount of your time. It was me who healed your family member. It was me who brought joy back to your child's heart. It is me, always and forever, loving you and yes, imagine, still ministering to you, always, always loving you no matter what you do, no matter how many times you fall, no matter how many times you forget me. Here and now, I love you.

There are many waiting for my healing touch, many waiting to hear my word ... the word that can melt their cold hearts, restore broken relationships, my word that can make all things new, my word that can bind up wounds, my word that can heal the mind, the body and the spirit. My people are in need and I wait. I wait for my word to go forth doing a mighty work through those I send into the world to speak, to heal, to comfort, to accompany, to love. You see, it's you who bring me to others, and so I say, job well done. Remember, every moment of every day I am working, I am moving in you.

You know love is giving when you think you have no more to give. Love is reaching out when you feel you have no strength yourself to help another. Love is giving until it hurts. Love is giving your time when your time is so precious and you have so much to do. Love is always giving, it's always patient, it's always kind, and love is humble. So be humble, be loving, be patient, be kind, but also, be aware, be aware always of those that would try to stifle the Spirit. And remember that I who am in you are far greater than he who is in the world and as long as you remember that, as long as you trust in my word, not in the words of others, then your heart will remain at peace for as you place your hope and your trust in my divine mercy, in my divine life, in my divine love, in my divine holy will, then your hearts will not be troubled regardless of what comes your way, for you know, nothing, absolutely nothing can happen without me allowing it to happen for a purpose.

So trust in me. I am the answer to all of your struggles and problems. I am the love that refused to die on the cross because of love of you. I would never have left you orphans. You are too weak. You would never have made it home to me, so I sent you another. I sent you my own Spirit to protect you, to guide you, to lead you, and to remind you of all the things that I said and did when I walked the earth. For I only said what I heard my Father saying. I only did what I saw my Father doing. And that is how you should respond in life ... do what you see me doing, speak as you hear me speaking, reach out, love, forgive. Forgiveness is a great gift. As you forgive, you will be forgiven. How often times you forget this. Forgive as I have forgiven you again and again and again, for you are my children and you must reflect my love in the world that is in such desperate need of the light, of the mercy, for I am the living God not a God of the dead but the God of the living here on earth and those who are around my throne. I will not leave you.

4/12/12

Continue to lift all of your priests up. Continue to pray for your priests. Tell them, tell them often of how they have helped you, blessed you, graced your life. There is enough people in the world that are trying to attack the Church, trying to destroy the Church. There are so many temptations in the world coming against my priests. They need your prayers. They need your steadfast prayers. There are many who have not remained faithful, but they are few in number. I tell you now to pray for your priests. They have temptations, worries, fears and anxieties of which you do not know.

They suffer loneliness, some of their own choosing. Many have no fellowship. Many are broken and many are hungering and thirsting for a deeper relationship with me. And it is your prayers, all of your prayers, that will fill their hearts with grace, with light. Many times, many times at the Eucharistic Celebration I see time and time again wounded hearts, broken hearts, yes even crushed spirits. And your prayers, your prayers my people, bring light to their darkness, bring peace to their turmoil, and bring love where they feel unloved. Little did you know, little could you guess. If there are priests that you are unhappy with, pray for them. Trust more in the power of prayer. Trust in my divine mercy. Trust in my love and pray for your priests.

To each of you I say this day that I have called you by name. I have called you particularly by your name. You know, even your name ... I placed your name in your mother's and father's hearts, and you don't like your name, but if you knew that it came from my heart to their hearts wouldn't you think it was beautiful? You see, I knew you and formed you in your mother's womb before you were even born, and it was me who breathed life into you ... "Ruah", the breath of life. I love you, each and every one of you. And some of you never give me a thought until trouble arises throughout the day. Do not wait my people, do not wait. The moment adversity enters your day immediately call upon my Holy Spirit. my Holy Spirit will give you light where there's darkness, will give you peace where there's turmoil, will give you wisdom when you are confused, will give you knowledge when you need wisdom and understanding. So do not wait, do not wait but turn to me.

I tell you this, it is a time of grace in the Church, it is a time of great mercy in the Church. I am raising up my people. I am calling them to be of one mind and one heart and one spirit. My call goes out to all, a call to holiness for all. Some will hear the call but will not heed the call. This is the power of prayer: through your prayers grace will be given to them to not only heed the call but to turn away from the things in the world that rob them of peace and grace. Through the power of your prayers grace will be given to enlighten their minds and their hearts and their understanding, and they will turn to me. Oh, you will be surprised, even shocked, and you won't even realize it was through the power of your prayers. So pray for those that you love. Pray for those who have wandered off. Pray for those who you think do not know me. Pray for all of the Church. A time of purging, a time of purification will come upon the Church but through your faithfulness, through your prayers, for your belief in divine mercy, grace will flow, and from glory to glory the Church will be renewed.

4/26/12 (1 of 2)

Do you not know yet? Have you not really understood that you are the "leaven." As I send you out into the world I call you to live in the world, but as I have told you in my Holy word to live in the world but not to be part of it. And I send each of you into the areas that I send you … the towns, the cities, the neighborhoods, the parishes, the families. I send you because you know and have experienced the power of the living God for you know that when you have been weak you have experienced my strength in you. So many have ears and do not hear. They have eyes and they do not see and their hearts have grown cold and hard. They have tried to sanitize their world. They've tried to sanitize their world in such a way that they have removed me from every aspect of their lives ... from their families, from their schools, in every aspect ... in politics and yes, so many even in the Church. They have forgotten who they are and who they've been called to be, to whom and for whom they've been consecrated.

But you must pray, you must pray for those who have fallen. You also must pray for the Church. You must pray for my vicar on earth. There will be much agony. Many will come against him. He will suffer much, but you see, I have sent him to be the one who would shepherd the Church through the storm. He is a man after my own heart. He is filled with truth, wisdom and great courage. He has put many in place who are filled with courage, who also know the truth so that they can also steer the Church in this time of turmoil in the storm.

And all of you, you're the "fisher", fishermen bringing other souls to me who would be lost if it were not for those who are filled with grace, filled with my Spirit, oh, weak as you are, but yet you search for truth even when things around you seem to be falling apart, even when circumstances in your lives bring you sorrow and pain, even when your family members can not understand from whence you come for they have turned their backs on the truth. But it is you, you who know the truth, you who have stood firm in the truth. It is you that I am raising up, each of you, to bring the message that this is indeed a time of great mercy, a time of mercy before justice is ushered in. I tell you now, you are sealed in my Spirit ... an indelible mark has been placed upon each of you and all those who believe. You will recognize one another for you will see me in each other, and you will recognize there is great work to do and you will labor for me. You will be light to them who are in darkness and you will point the way to my life that will feed and nourish them ... the bread that has come down from heaven. Yes, I am present in mind, in body and in spirit. You must bring this truth to others. You must let them know that I am calling each of them by name and allow them to see in you how I have healed your wounds, been your strength in weakness, your Savior in sin, your Lord and your God who has been manifested in so many ways in your lives. You are the "leaven." The Church will never ever be destroyed. You must take this message out so that they will have safe haven, that they can come and be filled with living water, that they might receive my life within them to sustain them, transform them, heal them and nourish them for the journey. Only you can answer ... will you go? Will you serve or will you sit idly by? Will you go and will you serve?

4/26/12 (2 of 2)

    I have seen your "yes." I read it in your heart. I also see the anticipation. I see even the anxiety ... what is it you want me to do Lord? I have placed you where I want you. I have called you by name and you have responded. Everyone has gifts. Everyone has talents. I ask you to use your gifts for one another so that my kingdom will receive glory. Do not worry about those that you love and who are far off. Didn't I tell you that you are "leaven?" There is no need to fear or to be anxious and certainly do not worry about tomorrow. Doesn't today have enough troubles of its own? Live with me in the present moment. If you stay in the heart of the Church, if you stay close to my own sacred heart I will set your hearts on fire and I will continue to breathe the breath of my Spirit upon you to accomplish the work that is still needed to be done. I will watch over you and protect you. Do not believe the things in the world that would try to frighten you, strike fear in your heart, in your spirit that is only to incapacitate you, but move forward. Go forth with your God for there is much for us to do ... me working in you and through you. Let not your heart be troubled. Do not fear or be dismayed. Every hair on your head is counted as I have told you. I will supply your needs. I will be your safe refuge. Do not be anxious and be not afraid for if I am with you who could be against you? Trust in my divine love. Trust in my merciful heart and come to the font of all mercy: to the sacrifice of the Mass, where you will receive strength and grace upon grace so that you will be transformed from glory to glory. Go often to the sacrament of

Reconciliation, a great gift of healing I have left within the Church, to receive healing balm, to receive grace and strength and courage, and above all, peace. Peace is my gift to you. The peace that I give you, if you keep your eyes and heart stayed on me, this peace will never leave you. When I breathed upon my Apostles did I not breathe peace on them before I even gave them their gifts? And so I have done with you ... I've given you peace. You must continue to grow in this peace so that you can continue to use the gifts that I have given to build up the kingdom. See, it's not your peace I strengthen, it's my peace I give to you.

5/3/12

You look around and you see the beauty of my creation. Many times when you are slow you take the time to admire the beauty, the colors, the change of the Season, the rains that water the earth and the sun that gives its rays, the moon that shines so beautiful in the evening and the glorious stars that light up the night. Yes, you have looked about and you have praised me when you have taken the time. This was all for you and yet my greatest creation is humanity.

You are above all things. I have told you in my Holy word you are above everything except the angels who are pure spirits. I've given you free will. And I ask you this night to ponder this thought: If your life was required this night, if you knew that this would be your last night, your last day on earth, how would you live it differently? Ponder it. Think deeply about it. Everyone lives their life like there is no end to the day. They live their life like there's no tomorrow. They try to get everything they want. They try to please their senses, and yet, do they not realize the greatest gift, do you not realize the greatest gift is your life, the life I have given to you freely with its challenges, with its trials, with its joys and triumphs, with its failures and its victories. I know exactly what to give you even though you question me time and time again ... Why is this happening? Why Lord have you allowed this? Lord, what purpose does this serve? Have you not yet understood, do you not yet comprehend that I have created all, I am Lord over all and that it is only through me, through the gift of my love and my life to you, my very breath. You see, if I called your spirit back now the tent would fold. The flesh is useless, but your spirit, the spirit that was created within you, was created in my likeness and in my image. Be concerned with your soul. Be concerned with your life. Be concerned that you have lived each day to the full. Savor moments of great joy and triumph. Savor the moments of sorrow and suffering for I give you exactly what you need even when you can not understand because you see, I am with you through it all, working all things together always for a greater good. That's why my love is a mystery. That's why my ways are not your ways. You want everything now and if you don't get it you think you're doing something wrong or someone else is. I am Lord over all. Nothing can happen without me allowing it for a purpose and a reason. So I ask you again: If your very life was required, how would you live the day? Would you make amends with those who have hurt you or you have wounded? Would you give more ... more of your time, more of your goods, more of your money, more of your gifts, more of your talents, or would you hoard them all to yourself? You see, I know you would want to give. I know that about you, you see. But you do not know that each day is a gift as if there were no other gifts, no other days and that's what you have to come to understand. You have to comprehend that truth that everyday is a gift. There's nothing you can do to earn it. It is my gift to you and that's the gift you must offer back to me: your life. I ask you, I do not demand. I call you to remember who you are: children of the Most High God, and reflect that in everything you do. And when you fall and falter along the way you only need to look to me, to call my name. Even in the midst of temptation the Devil will flee. In the deepest of sorrows I will give you my joy. Ponder this thought and think deeply on it. If your very life was required how would you live it out that final day, and then try to the best of your ability to live that way from this day forth each day. Be fed and nourished at my table. Be healed and empowered through the sacrament of Confession. I have not left you nor abandoned you nor will I ever. I will be there to minister to your every need and I have so much to give you, more than you're really willing to accept. Ponder the thought. Think deeply on it. How would you live your life if this was the last day of your life, and then begin to live every day that you have as a gift in that manner.

5/17/12

I summoned you and you have responded. You have opened your heart to my Holy Spirit. Others are called but they are not open to receive the outpouring of my Holy Spirit. So often they are struck with fear, curiosity, and they wonder what it is that they would have to give up? What would the Lord ask of each who would dare to enter into the deep? That's the main question in their heart even when they do not voice it. How much of myself will I have to give up? How much of my life will I have to surrender? What are the things that the Lord would take from me? And they miss, they miss the beauty and the gifts ... the most wonderful gift of my Spirit. That's why I say time and time again that my perfect love casts out all fear. My Spirit is outpoured not to change everyone, you see I created you in my likeness, in my image. I created you out of the desire of my own heart. You were conceived in my mind before you were conceived in your mother's womb. I knew you, I loved you and I breathed life into you.

But you see, you were still in awe ...awe of me, awe of your triune God, until you began to realize a little bit more each day. Leaving me and entering into the world you began to realize the things that you wanted even as a baby. When you cried your loving parents would try to tend to your needs. So even as a baby each day you grew a little further away, then you became a little child and again, you forgot a little bit more of who I am, and then you became a young adult and each one of you, each and every one of you in your journey of life so far have yielded and surrendered, fallen back, gotten up and tried again because you have experienced, you have tasted and seen the goodness of the Lord. You will not be deprived. But others are still afraid. Others do not know that my love is not to change, simply to help them become who they really are, created in my likeness, created in my image.

And so I say to you tonight, you have blessed the Lord by your acquiescence and to the promptings of my Spirit in your life. I called and you responded to the call. I called you closer and you drew closer. I've called you by name and now at this point of your journey I want to deepen your walk in the Spirit. You see, the gift of my Spirit is about transforming you from glory to glory, transforming you into receiving the power that has been available to you since your baptism, the authority that I had given you through the sacramental life of the Church through Baptism and your Confirmation. Through the sacraments that you have received, you have received grace from on high ... the grace to transform, the grace to heal, the grace to know, the grace to be, not necessarily to do. But again I call you a little deeper because I want to continue to allow you to grow into all that I've called you to be. I want you to experience my power and my authority and when you do more fully you will grow more perfectly in love and it will be this love, my love in you and through you, that will change the world. Love is holiness my children. Love is giving not taking. Love is self-sacrificing. Love is always looking to the good of the other that's why I want you to grow more fully into my Spirit. Come a little deeper into the living waters. This is what I call you to so that your life might be filled with my joy ... my joy at work in you to give you that peace that the world can never rob you of regardless of circumstances. This is my desire to give you the desires of your heart. So be at peace and know that I have loved you with an everlasting love.

5/31/12 (1 of 2)

I call each of you, each of you, not some of you, not a few of you, but all of you ... my people. I call you to invoke the power of my Spirit at all times. When you make a decision, invoke the power of my Holy Spirit to give you the wisdom and discernment and knowledge that you need to make a decision in right judgment, to be prudent when necessary. Invoke my Holy Spirit at all times before you pray, yourself or with others. Invoke my Spirit when you lay hands on others. Invoke my Holy Spirit to well up within you dispelling your own anxieties, your fears and your doubts. That is indeed why I told my own Apostles and the disciples to wait for the promise. If they needed to wait for the fulfillment of the Father's promise which was the Holy Spirit to come upon them so that they would be filled with power, do you think you wouldn't need that gift so that you can move in the power of my Spirit?

My Spirit does sanctify in the fire of my love, burning away everything that is not of me, and the warmth of my love draws others to me through you, through the fire of my love burning in you. As I have told you I am a consuming fire. I consume all that is not of me and burn it away and I consume all of you who allow me to possess you. You know, you don't possess the Holy Spirit. It's the Holy Spirit who possesses each one of you. As you open your heart and your mind and your spirit I would have you be where I am and you could not get there on your own. You could not accomplish the works that I did and far more than these without the power of the Holy Spirit because it would be the Spirit of the living God, my Spirit that is left with you, that would teach you, reveal to you, sanctify you so that you could grow more perfectly in love, for am I not love itself?

Love continues to sacrifice. Love continues to give without counting the cost. How much have you loved lately? How much have you thought of others before yourself? Love is giving your time when you really don't have time to give. Love is giving your patience to those who surround you and frustrate you. Love is forgiving even when you have not been the cause or the problem of the argument, the dispute, the wound. Love gives, it does not take and it is only through the sanctification by the power of my Spirit working in you and through you, my consuming fire, that will allow you to burn for me igniting a heart with my love through a spark of your own heart, of your own love for me.

Once again, I have placed you where I want you. You are growing in me and I am working in you. I have called you to follow me and you took the courage of that first step and many thereafter. I will bless your "yes". Remember, the things that you fear the most, they're not from me. My perfect love wants to cast out that fear. My perfect love wants to give you peace. My perfect love wants to form you in my likeness and image, grace upon grace, glory upon glory ... transformation, day in and day out. This is why I left my Spirit with you. This is why my Spirit is indeed the very soul of the Church. I left you my body and blood to feed you and nourish you and to give you my life, but I left my Spirit, the very soul of the Church, so that the Church and her mission would be carried out. Without the Holy Spirit the mission can not be accomplished. You are part of that mission, but you need to call upon my Holy Spirit. You need to invoke my Spirit to lead you into all that is right, good and holy.

5/31/12 (2 of 2)

Be on your guard. Guard your heart, your mind and your spirit for the Deceiver is running rampant ... the father of lies. I tell you to be on your guard. Let not your ears be tickled. There is not an "American" Church. There is only one, holy, catholic and apostolic Church. Where Peter is, there I am. I tell you to stand in solidarity with the holy father. I tell you to pray for your shepherds for there is a battle going on and I call you to intercede. I call you to intercede for my beloved priests. The Holy Father will suffer much. Do not let him suffer alone but stand with him. Let your voices be heard. Let your fidelity be known so that you will not be led astray. Remember, where Peter is, there I am.

6/7/12

You praised and thanked me for the gift of my Precious Body and Blood ... the Holy Eucharist. It is in my Precious Body and Blood that you will find the fullness of salvation because you see, as you eat my body and drink my blood I unite myself with you and we become intimate. We become one through the power of my Spirit at work in you and through you, and the more you eat my body and drink my blood, the more you will remember my death and resurrection. It will always be on your mind, on your lips, and in your heart. That is why I feed you. That is why with the chalice of my blood I wash you, strengthen you, continue to draw you deeper into my own heart, continue to fill you with wisdom and knowledge and grace and understanding, just to name a few of the beautiful gifts that I give to you. As you eat my body and drink my blood I draw you into a deeper intimate relationship with myself.

You know, when I place friends in your life, a friend that I give you is a friend forever. A friend that I give you is a treasure. Remember this ... a treasure indeed to take care of, protect and cherish. I know all about friendship you see because I call you friends. I call you each a friend and friendship in me will draw you deeper and deeper into the mysteries of the triune God ... of Father and Son and Holy Spirit. I draw together the truth of the Church being ever "ancient", but ever "new". Did I not draw together the Passover from the ancient and the new covenant of my body and blood in the New Covenant? You see, they are not separate but linked together because I was the perfect sacrifice. I am the perfect sacrifice. And then every time you eat my body and drink my blood, you are at the foot of the cross, you are right there, right there at Calvary. I was the perfect sacrifice … no need ever again, the sacrifice was fulfilled. I offered myself in obedience to the Father, perfect obedience.

And the devil is a liar. He's the father of lies. He's a deceiver and he would have you believe that it's just a story not relevant today. But I tell you this, that is such a deceit, that any who believe that are on the road to perdition. They're on the road to damnation. And so it is through you who know the truth to share that truth, to love the sinner enough to warn them in love. Tell them about my great mercy. Tell them about the grace of the sacramental life of the Church.

I call you to confession. I call you to experience grace upon grace so that you would begin to understand the mystery of my love, that the more you avail yourself to the power of my healing love in the sacrament of forgiveness, the sacrament of love and mercy, the more you avail yourself to the power of forgiveness and healing, the more power you will have available to you.

So as you eat my body and drink my blood I will remain in you and work through you as you have my friendship and you have friendship in me. Remember, it is a gift freely given, no way can you earn it. I just call you to bear fruit that will last and that is by going out and sharing this truth with others. There is an urgency, I say it again, an urgency to allow the truth to flow out of you so that other souls may be set free. Not in condemnation I ask you to speak, not harshly and not even in judgment. Strictly speak the truth in love. This is what makes the difference. Be at peace my friend. Remember I always call you friends.

6/14/12

So many of you who have felt battered, worn, beat up ... count yourself as being blessed. Although you do not understand it at the time, you have been battered and beaten by the storms of life. But it is through this battering, it is through the storms that come in and out of your life that I make you "sea-worthy". I allow the salt water to flow over you so that you can really become that "salt", the salt to make others thirst for the living God, the salt that I call you to be to the world, that is one who has been battered, torn, worn, broken down. It is that one when he stands firm in faith, it is that one when she holds on to her faith, it is then that you are becoming sea-worthy, like a good captain on a ship.

You see, my ways are not your ways. I have said this time and time again. But the person who stands firm in the midst of adversity, in the midst of trials, in the midst of testing and temptation, this is the person I choose to carry on the missions, to carry on my work. But for every storm in the sea no matter how high the waves of the storm are, no matter how rocky the water becomes, if you focus on the light, my light, the light of Christ shining brightly through the storm, I will guide you, protect you, watch over you and draw you gently, gently into the light to dispel the darkness that surrounds you at those times. A light house out in the deep, time and time again has shown the way to safe haven. The light shining brightly in the darkness guides and leads to a port of comfort. This is what I do for you when you focus on me, the light of the world. When you focus on me you have no time to focus on all that's going on around you.

Trust me day by day, moment by moment. There's nothing you can do to change what happened yesterday or the day before or the past. You can not even do anything about the future. Do you not realize that yet? All you can do is be open in the present so that I can guide you and lead you and direct you. Let go of the past. Do not hold on to what has been but focus on what you have now in the present moment which is much more than many of your fellow people have. You have much. I have blessed you with much. Do not worry what has been taken away or what is gone. Focus on what you have now for whatever you have given up, whatever you have lost in the past, I promise you I will bless you a hundred fold with so much more.

Battered and worn and beaten though you might feel at times, you will be getting stronger, you will become more aware of the power of my Spirit at work in you. You will become more aware that I alone am in control of all things. No one or no thing is greater than my power and my divine will. Everyone has a choice: my will, your will … my will, their will. Where do you stand? Will you allow me to continue my work in you to become all that I call you to be, and that's a light shining brightly in the darkness?

6/21/12 (1 of 2)

You know, I have called you by name. I've called you here this night at this time so that I could love you, love you into wholeness. You know, I know you better than anyone else. I know you better than you know yourself, after all, I knew you before you were even in your mother's womb. I know the deepest recesses of your heart. I know your wounds, your scars. I know the heart that has loved much and has not always been loved in return. Oh, I can understand that, for it was my heart, my heart that was pierced for love of you. It was my heart that loves and surrendered in obedience to my Father ... my Father and your Father. I know you well. I know the deepest recesses of your being. I even know what makes you tick when you wonder why you do what you do. Do you think I don't understand? Do you think I don't know? Do you think I don't care about the burdens that you carry or the sorrows that you have? I assure you, I am greater than every problem, every sorrow, every ounce of turmoil. I am greater than it all.

That's why I called you here this night so that you could be filled with a peace, my peace I give you. It's a peace not as the world gives it as you know, but a peace that I myself will give you, and from this night forward I will draw you deeper and closer to my own heart. I will nourish you, heal you, strengthen you and give you exactly what you really need, not necessarily what you want. Yes indeed, I know everything about you.

I want you to experience my love, a love that will ask nothing from you, a love that will not take but a love that will give. I will strengthen your willpower. I will strengthen your resolve. I will strengthen your heart for you are weary and restless. But today, hearing my voice today, offers you hope. As you place your hope and your trust in me, I will fill you with everything that you need. You will lack nothing ... not strength, not courage, not grace nor any material thing. I will supply each and every one of your needs. Rest in me. Be at peace in me for I will make all things new and I will raise you. I will raise you above the mire. I will raise you above the turmoil. I will raise you above the anger, the resentment and the bitterness because I will fill you with my peace, my grace, my joy and my courage.

    I want you to come away with me. I want you to come away with me to a quiet place where I can speak to your heart, where I can refresh and renew your soul and spirit where I will be transforming you by the renewal of your mind. Come on ... come away with me. Find a quiet place so that we can be.

6/21/12 (2 of 2)

    I have called you by name, I say it again, I have called you by name. I have placed that name in the hearts of your parents who named you for this is the name that when I call to you, you will respond to. Be still and listen. In the silence of your heart you will truly hear me speak. By name I have called you. Out of the depth of my love I have formed you and placed you in your mother's womb. You are mine, never doubt, you are mine.

6/28/12

The faith that I have given you is truly a gift. The faith that I have given you is a gift from my Spirit. I've given you this faith so that you can grow, grow in the spirit, grow into what I'm calling you to be ... salt to the earth, salt to all those who do not know me, who have yet to believe ... some willfully so, others who's hearts have grown cold, and still others who do not understand the magnificent gift of my love. So this gift that I have given to you, given freely I might add, there's nothing you could do to earn it, it's purely a gift from my heart to your heart. And because you have willingly received it, because you have held on to me even in times of testing, even in times of heartache and trouble and trials, because of this your faith is growing, because of this you are growing more perfectly into my likeness and my image.

I have blessed you. I have called you here. I speak to each of your hearts, to each and every one of your hearts because you are mine. I would not have you despair. I would not have you loose focus on the truth. I would not have you be so saddened by the events that have come about and more to come ... this great purging of the Church, the purging of your Country. Never loose focus of me. Do you doubt? Do you still have doubts within you that "I am"? Before all things came to be, I am. I am the resurrection and the life. I am the way. There is no other way, though many times you try to find another way. I alone am the way. I'm the truth and life.

And so this gift of faith, I call you to cherish it. I call you to safeguard this rich deposit of faith that has been given to you and handed down to you ... why ... because others will try to rob you of it by many different words, many different wiles, many different circumstances. They will try to rob you of the great gift that you have received. But you see, that's not the reality. With all the words that they speak, it's not reality. With all the persuasion of their words, it is not reality. And though they speak with a tongue that seems pleasing to the ear, they come from the father of lies. And so I say to you, do not be dismayed, do not be sad, and certainly do not be confused for all is under my control. I have the power to loose and to bind. I have the power to raise you up.

And for all those who will not receive the power of my love, they have chosen to walk away, they have not believed nor have they received ... they have made their choice. But while there is still time I call you, I call you to make a difference in the world. I call you to stay focused on me, to walk in my way, to walk in my truth, to listen to my word for my word will be a lamp to your feet. You will follow that light and you will walk in light and not in darkness. You will be filled with truth and not a lie and as you grasp that truth, as you grasp that mission to know that I am the God of the impossible ... when you fully comprehend that truth that there is no other way that leads to eternal life, no other way, I am indeed the way.

And so I ask you to focus on me. I ask you to call to me day in and day out because as you touch me, touch my heart, touch my life, I fill you with my love, I fill you with my life. Every time then that you eat my body and drink my blood you will have my life within you. I am victory itself, everything else is a lie. It comes from the father of lies. No matter how nicely or how packaged it becomes, it is still a lie. But you know the truth and the truth will set you free. Speak my truth so others might come to believe.

7/12/12

You are learning, slowly but ever so surely. You are learning to trust me. You are learning more and more each day that when you call to me I will come to you. You are learning to trust me even when you are pretty sure that I'm not going to be able to do the things that you want done. Your way and my way ... isn't that always a struggle? But I told you that I am the only way and the more you trust me, the more you trust in my love, the more you trust in my divine providence, the more you will come to understand my love, my provision, my joy ... the joy that I give to you ... my joy. And so often you do not experience my joy because you're worrying, you're frustrated, you doubt, you fear, even times you are confused. Sometimes I need to shake things up a bit to get your attention, to let you know that I am with you at all times, that I watch you ... your comings and your goings ... that I minister to you. Yes, I minister to you even when you're not aware of it. You think that it is your own will, your own triumphs, your own efforts, your own skills that bring about the situations and the circumstances in your life that give you peace, that bring about the situations and circumstances in your life that you think you worked out so perfectly when, in fact, it is me working all things out. It is me working all things together. It is me. And the more you become aware of that fact, the more you will begin to trust me. Oh, you'll trust me in the beginning with little things, and then when you begin to realize that it is I, it is the Lord in your midst, then you will trust me a little more each day. But trust is a growth process. It doesn't happen all at once. It's not one size fits all.

I measure, I weigh every single cross that comes into your life, then I fill you with the grace to carry each cross, and it is through the cross that you are redeemed day in, day out. You see, I have loved you with an everlasting love. I am loving you even when you feel it not. I am speaking to your heart to guide you, to lead you, to direct you even when you do not have ears to hear or a heart to receive because you're preoccupied with the ways of the world. I often wish that you would listen to me as often as you listen to the things that are going on in the world because you see it's those things that rob you of peace. It's those things in the world and of the world that disturb you, confuse you. It is Satan's way of robbing you of peace.

You know, it's not a myth. It's not a story nor a fable. Satan is real. He just creates an artificial reality ... artificial as he tries to copy, copy my power, copy my strength. But again I say it is a false reality. It's a false perception that he shows you in the world. He comes to rob and to deceive and yes, to set you on a path that would lead you away from me. Oh, things sound good. They even feel good, but the outcome is evil, the outcome brings destruction.

And so I say to you now, you have heard my word, you have acted on my word … I tell you to be aware, to be wise so that you will not be led astray. I want you to remember that I do not send you alone into the world and I do not send you out into the world alone. I bring others into your life to accompany you along the path, the journey called "life." The evil one is cunning but I tell you he is only an imitation, an imitation of my power, an imitation of my strength, an imitation of joy. It is not reality.

I am alone. There is no other God. "I Am", and I tell you now to be on your guard, to be wise with the wisdom from above and trust only in my ways. They might not seem to be the ways of the world. They might not seem to be your ways, but my way is perfect and my way leads to salvation. And so I ask you to continue to trust me. Trust me on the way as I anoint you and empower you to go out and bring the good news to others. I call you to be aware of my power, my authority, and my presence in your life.

All the stories in the Scriptures about healing … why do you think they're there? They're there to show for every generation that I am a God who is Lord over every circumstance, every illness, every disease, every circumstance. I have given you that power of the resurrection to come against evil and fear not for I alone am the only reality you need. Did I not rob Satan of all his power? Did I not strip him of every ounce of power? He holds no power over you. I do not understand why so many fear him. I do not understand why so many tremble at his name when it should be my name that others tremble at, for I am an awesome God. I am a God filled with a fire and the power that no other has. There is only one God ... the Father who loved you so much that I did not leave you to your own wiles but sent my only beloved Son into the world for each of you, to die that you might live. And then my Son could not bear to part from you and so He left you His Spirit to bring my healing power, my authority, my strength, my forgiveness, my divine mercy, and on and on it goes, bringing my love, my presence into the world that is in so desperate need of my love and my mercy and my peace.

Do not look at the circumstances of the world and fear, but continue to praise my holy name for it is only by the cross and by my holy name and by the shedding of my precious blood that redemption will come. All I ask of you is to be prepared. All I ask of you is your "yes" and I will do the rest.

7/19/12

Often times you wonder, you wonder whether you're growing in my Spirit, and sometimes you never even give it a thought and those are the times that you're floundering. I would tell you to be aware, always be aware of the power of my Spirit in your life. Always be aware that Satan comes to rob, to steal, to destroy. He comes to take away your peace and to fill you with a lie, an illusion. My word when spoken, your faith when shared, brings forth much fruit. Although Satan can manifest in many different ways an imitation of my gifts, they are just that, an imitation of the gifts of my Spirit. However, the gift of my Spirit living in you, at work in you, brings forth and bears fruit and that's the only way fruit will last by yielding to the gifts of my Spirit at work in your life ... not an imitation.

You must be authentic. If you profess yourself as my follower, my disciple, my ambassador, my representative, then you will know that you are growing when you reflect the character, the likeness, the image of the Triune God: Father and Son and Holy Spirit. All else is an imitation. But a true follower of mine, an authentic reflection representative of my love, is one that bears fruit and that's how others can look and see if you are really walking in the fullness of your dignity as a Christian. If you are yielding to the grace of your Baptism, if you are open to the power of my Spirit strengthened within you at Confirmation, look only to the gifts of my Spirit and as they flow out of you all who come to know you will see that you are bearing the fruit from the tree of life: peace and love and joy, forgiveness and mercy and understanding, wisdom and knowledge and purity. You will reflect more and more the dignity of your personhood ... a person that has been delivered out of darkness into my glorious light.

I ask you to be aware of the grace of the sacraments. The more you stay away from the sacrament of confession the weaker you become. You see, I am there to heal. I am there to forgive. I am there to fill you with grace and strength and courage because you see, apart from me you can bear no fruit that will last. But when you live in me and allow me to work in you and through you, others will be drawn to you not because of you but because of me in you. You will be a joy to be around. You will bring peace wherever you go because you will bring me and I will reach others through you.

You have heard it said this night that one who was lost was found through grace, through my daughter sharing the truth of faith … brought one back to the sacrament of confession. *(A prayer group member had just testified of witnessing to a person who had been away from the Church and sacraments for many years and the person has come back).* Love covers a multitude of sin. So I tell you this day, be aware of the power of my Spirit in you so that you can give others the beautiful gift of my Spirit at work in your life so that they too can walk in the fullness of the dignity of their own baptism. I have saved … this is true. The gift of salvation is free but one has to be open to receive it.

8/16/12

If I who come to you and speak to you, speak my words to you … my word that strengthens and heals, my word that sets free and delivers, my word that edifies, my word that encourages, my word that exhorts … if I who speak to you in all these many ways and more still, don't you feel liberated? Don't you feel at peace? Don't you feel enthused? Don't you feel strengthened? Don't you have confident assurance when I speak to you, when I reveal the mysteries of my heart to your heart? Think on that, ponder that, and think how others feel when I speak through you. Let your mind absorb this truth. You see, when I speak through you, when you allow me to use you, then I bring those same comforts, those same gifts of peace and healing and deliverance, exhortation, forgiveness and love and mercy ... I bring them to others through you. Think how they feel. They feel the way you feel when I do that to you. So I encourage you to speak my word when necessary. Be my example at all times for they are watching. Others are watching to see if you are a credible witness, to see if your words line up to your actions. I say this to you that you can begin to comprehend how simply I move in you and through you. So many try to complicate me but I am in all purity, in all power, in all tenderness and gentleness, but with a fierce power that is above every power.

And you see, I have left my Spirit with you to help you to recognize and understand that I fight for you. The battle is mine, not yours. The battle is mine. I have left my Spirit with you to remind you of this so that I would be working in you and through you at all times as my Holy Spirit reminds you of all that I said, all that I did. How quickly my people forget. And yet with a gentle reminder they are once again filled with enthusiasm. Don't walk away. Don't separate yourself but come to me. Come to me especially through the gifts that I have given to you ... the gifts that I have revealed to your heart, the gifts that I have made manifest so that you might grow into all that I call you to be.

I tell you to come to eat my body and to drink my blood for then my life will be in you, the more you come, the more you come to be one with me in Holy Communion. When you talk to me and I talk to you in these quiet moments I am never so close as I am then, so speak to me from your heart. Hold nothing back. Tell me freely your thoughts, your feelings, your fears, your anxieties, your hopes and desires. Tell me all for I am your all in all. So as you eat my body and drink my blood remember this: Do not eat and partake of my body and blood as you would a meal under ordinary circumstances. You eat, you chat, you talk, you read the paper, you have conversation with not a thought of what is going into your body. When you eat my body and drink my blood do it with zest and zeal. Devour the gift that I have given you because you see, this food is my life, my life in you, God in you. Imagine that! Ponder that, so that when you come to my banquet table you will see me in a new way as giving you truly my own life ... God within.

9/6/12

My word indeed is living. My word is spoken and it brings forth life because of the breath of my Spirit. I have left you Mother Church. Just as I came from my own mother's womb through the power of the Holy Spirit over shadowing my mother, so too the same Holy Spirit has been given to each of you through your baptism … the Spirit of the living God dwelling in you. When the word is heard, the Scriptures proclaimed, my Spirit hovers over the word that is spoken as you receive it into your heart. My word is living through my Spirit in you, with you, and through you, and as I hover over the word as it's proclaimed, it is to give you a new understanding to truth, day in and day out, if you have ears to hear and a heart to receive.

I have given you much. I have blessed my people mightily. I have enriched your life in many, many ways. All that you have, you know, comes from me. All good things come from me. What do you do with the good that I give you? I give you these things, the goodness from the heart of God, to your hearts … the gift of grace so that that grace might be manifested in the hearts of all those that you come in contact with. My word is living and the waters of my Spirit well up within you so that you might allow my love, the living water of my love, to drench all those that you come in contact with. Do you think I search far and wide for you alone to save you, to draw you deep into the depths of my own love and heart, to teach you, to guide you, to strengthen you when you are weak? Do you think I do it just for you? I do it for others so that you might be a gift of living water, a gift of light to dispel the darkness. I challenge you. I challenge each of you this night to hold fast to this truth that you hear. Ponder it in your heart and then act upon it. Just as my mother heard the word proclaimed and acted on it, so too I call you to act on this word. This is an urgent message. Let your ears be attuned. Let your heart receive it. I have left my Spirit with you, each of you, to guide you, to lead you to all truth. I have left you Mother Church to guide you as a mother guides her children.

I place before you life and death, instructed you to choose life that you might live. Where sin abounds I assure you that grace abounds ever more so. Those that will choose to walk away from truth, who choose to walk away from the life I have placed before them, they are left to their own wiles, they will bring about destruction on themselves. But you, you who have heard my word and taken it into your heart and your being, you know the truth. But to those who walk away, who choose to turn their back on me, to those who make the personal decision to go on a different path than the one I have placed before them, then woe to them and woe to all those who lead them astray. I tell you this night that you must speak the truth whether it's convenient or inconvenient, whether it's popular or not. All will be called to an accounting. How well did they love and did they take my love, my mercy, my grace, my strength, my healing love and compassion to the people who are most in need, or were they silent so that evil could triumph? Let your ears hear. Let your heart receive, for it is you that I have found my pleasure in. And all those who hear my word, who keep my word and who act on my word, I am well pleased. I ask you to go out and spread the seed of faith to all that you come in contact with. I myself will water the seed. It doesn't depend on you, you see, it depends on me … but I work through you.

9/20/12

    Just as in your everyday life, whether you're walking or driving or however you choose to move from one place to another, I give you instructions. A red light would, of course, tell you to stop. A yellow informs you to move with caution. A green light would tell you to proceed. When there's danger ahead ... a curve, a bend in the road ... I inform you so that you might be prepared, and so too it is this way in life. So many times day in and day out I send you warnings of what is ahead. So many times I tell you to be cautious and other times I show you that it's a place that you should proceed and go forth. These are evil times that you are living in. There is much darkness at hand. Many have run the red lights, many have thrown caution to the wind, and many have refused to move but stay stuck in the dirt, the mire, the sin.

    I have sent you my Mother. I have sent her time and time again to bring the message of my constancy but also of the urgency at hand. Once again, many have chosen to continue in their wicked ways. Many still have gone forward without any signs of caution thinking they are in charge of their own destiny. I have shown each of you, I have shown every one of you what is required to live eternally ... eternally. You were created as eternal beings and I have said that the choice is yours whether you live eternally in the darkness or you live eternally in glory with me forever. Many have lost their way and will allow no one to help them, not even me. They have shut their heart and built walls around it. They have closed their ears to the truth and they refuse to recognize and see the signs that I have placed before them, and so I come through you. I continue to send signs, signs of the times, and so many refuse to hear or see. But you, yes you, you I have brought to a safe haven. You I have nourished and fed solid food. Put away childish things for I call you to grow in the Spirit of my love that your heart and your mind would be opened and pure and transparent so that my light might shine brightly through you for those who are in darkness, and my light shining through you will be a beacon of hope for those in darkness.

I tell you to be prepared. I tell you to place your hope, your trust, your families, your businesses, and yes, your Country, in my care. You have eyes, you do not see, ears, you do not hear, and many wander away from me. But this is a time, this is a time to go out in holy boldness and bring the good news that will set my people free. I have placed before you two roads: one that I call my people to travel on, the other that will lead to perdition. As I have told you, you will choose. Be prepared to accept the consequences of your choices. You see, I have told you that many people think that I am dead, many others think that I am a ploy of the imagination, many still think I do not exist. Woe to them! You … in you, they can find me. In you they can come to believe in me. Allow your light to shine brightly in the darkness and let nothing, nothing frighten you. Let nothing stifle you. Focus on me and keep your eyes on the very source of your life. I will watch over and protect my own. Did I not tell my beloved that I have gone to prepare a place for you so that where I am you too will be. Bring this message of eternal life to others. Go in boldness to proclaim the truth that will set my people free.

10/4/12

You know, I call each of you in a very special way. As I said many times, I actually summon you here. My word goes out and summons each of you to come. To come and to gather in my name to be formed and transformed through my Spirit and to be made holy as I am holy through the washing of your hearts and your minds and your spirits through my word. I remind you that you can have no life, no life within you, unless you eat my body and drink my blood because it is my life, eternal life, that enters in you and transforms your heart, your mind, your spirit more perfectly into my likeness and my image.

There are many who are waiting and watching, waiting and watching before they make that commitment to come and follow me. Many who are, indeed, watching you to see what is the cost of this discipleship I call you to. How much are you willing to give of yourself? How much are you willing to surrender to me? Will you surrender your children, your grandchildren? You see, they were mine before they were yours. Your mate ... you see, it is I who have given you your helpmate. It is I who have given you your mate as head of your home as well, and so I tell you to cherish the gift that comes from my heart to your heart. The roll of every wife is to draw her husband closer to the heart of God so that he might enter eternal life, and so too it is with the husband. He must love his wife as I love the Church, my bride. He must be willing to sacrifice everything for her so that he will be able to help her along the path of salvation to enter into eternal life.

But each of you have a role of discipleship. A roll that is my plan, not your plan ... no, my plan for your lives. How many times have you said "who would have thought" and see, it was I who thought. "Who could ever imagine this?" You see, it was conceived in my mind. I have told you that your thoughts and my thoughts are very different. My thoughts are far above your thoughts, but I ask you to trust me. I ask you just to trust me a little bit more every moment than you did the moment before. Often times you are stressed out filled with anxieties and fears of the present day. But you see, as you stay focused on me, as you allow me to live in you, all those fears, those anxieties, those traumatic experiences that life brings ... you see, you would have peace in the midst of them if you allow me to reign as Lord over your family, your business ... if you would allow me to be Lord over your decisions.

Many are watching to see indeed, what was the cost of your discipleship? You see, they're already making excuses of what it will cost them and so, therefore, they will not follow me. And so they must see in you a joy that can not be described in the human language. They must see in you a peace that goes beyond all understanding. They must see in you a love that loves at all times. They must see in you a heart that is filled with compassion and mercy for then they will begin to hunger and thirst for righteousness. That's what discipleship is all about and I have called each of you to go and make disciples without counting the cost. I will empower you beyond your imagination. I will fill you with the fire of my divine love that will melt the coldest hearts. Discipleship ... that's what I call you to. Be my disciples, and then go ... go therefore and make new disciples in my name by the fire and power of my Spirit.

10/11/12

So many today talk about the darkness. They talk of the evil that has penetrated this world. They talk about the tumultuous times that they are living in. They talk about their fears and their anxieties and so many grow despondent, so many are without hope, so many are bound-up through addictions ... many, many addictions. And I want to remind each of you that although there has been an unleashing into the world of angels of darkness, I assure you, I tell you ... I want you to understand, for every angel of darkness, I have sent an angel of light into the world to fight the battles so you don't have to. They are fighting for my people ... sons and daughters after my own heart. People who are called by my name. And I send my angels to do battle with the angels of darkness so that my people would be led in times of need to safety so that my angels will guide and lead you in a path of righteousness for my namesake, for my name is above every other name. Who do you place your hope and your trust in? Trust in my name. All of your angels behold my holy face and so too I call each of you to be aware that you have nothing to fear, nothing to be afraid of. Do not at any time curse the darkness. Only look to me, the light of the world, to shed light to dispel the darkness.

Oh, you are living in troubled times, but did you expect anything less? For those who know my word, for those who prepare their hearts, for those who look to my coming, in my time, in my way, you should be looking and having your eyes adjusted to the light that will indeed dispel every darkness. Every dark act will be brought into the light. All those fears, all those anxieties about doom and gloom … put no faith in them. I alone know the hour and the time, but I have told you to be aware, to be prepared for the times that are coming … actually already upon you.

But you, you will be ministers of my love and mercy. You will be ministers in my name that is above every name … every name of every sickness, every name of every addiction, every name of every demon. I the Lord your God am holy, and because I am holy I have called each of you by name to share in that holiness, to be set apart, to be holy and set apart … to be a contradiction to the world at hand.

I will rip down walls that many have spent years building around their hearts. I will awaken minds through the gift that I will send: a gift of light, a gift of mercy, and many will come to believe who never did before. So do not fear. This is a time of great mercy and that is why I need my warriors, that is why I raise you up. I raise you up that you might bring to those in darkness my light. I raise you up so that you might speak the truth when lies surround so many. I have raised you up because, again, you are children, my children ... flesh of my flesh and bone of my bone. So continue to stand in the gap for all those who you love and pray for so that they will not be "victims" but "victors" through the power of your prayer, through the example of your lives. I make the crooked way straight and where there is no way I will make a way. So let not your heart be troubled. Have faith in me and know that I will never leave you nor forsake you.

10/18/12 (1 of 2)

You speak of my love and you speak of my mercy, and rightly so, but do you really have a grasp, a real understanding of my love and my mercy? My love has the power to transform, the power to take pride and mold it into humility. The power of my love can thaw the coldest of hearts as my love radiates from my heart to their hearts to your heart. My love indeed is all powerful and all transforming.

You pray for your loved ones. You want them to come to know me and love me and serve me. You want them to come and follow me. You want them to walk in my way. You want them to experience the truth ... my truth. I am truth itself for I alone am the way, the truth and the life. You want all these good things for your children, for your mates, for your siblings, for your extended family and friends, and this is really the desire of your heart. I alone know the desire of each and every one of your hearts before you even lift a prayer to me. But know this, know this about my love and my divine mercy: As you pray, as you stand steadfast in the gap for those who are away from me, those who have fallen from grace, those who are confused and have chosen a different way, those who have not known the truth and so you are afraid that their souls would be lost, I say to you continue to pray for you see, as you pray, as these prayers go up like incense before my throne, then the power of grace is released and flows from my heart to the hearts of those that you are praying for. And as you continue to pray, as the incense of prayers go up, know that the power of my Spirit is being moved through the gift of prayer. My Spirit will fall upon those who you are praying for and I will continue to move and to call. I will tug at their heart, their mind, their spirit. I will begin to move in their lives in such a way that the grace that falls from heaven from the power of those prayers issuing up to heaven, they will meet and they will be manifested in the lives of those you are praying for.

      Do not be of little faith. Do not think for a moment that your prayers are in vain, and begin with yourself. Do you think that I who am, do you think that I who created you, formed you, filled you with the Spirit of my life, do you think that I would see my own children lost? Do you think for one moment that I would not leave all to find those who are lost, not because they reject me but because they do not understand. And because you have interceded, because your prayers went up like incense, my grace flows out upon all you're praying for. Again I say begin with yourself. You do not see the goodness within yourself. I give you gifts of leadership, service, peace, joy, power, authority. I give you so much and yet you continue to beat yourself up, continue to think yourself unworthy. My children, all are unworthy, that's why I came into the world to redeem you. So because of my love, because of my power, because of my redeeming love, you too, you too reflect my likeness and my image. Do not, do not take that gift for granted. I am drawing you day in and day out. I am drawing you deeper into the Spirit of my love. I am transforming you. I'm changing lives. I'm moving mountains that you do not even recognize are being moved because of your faith. Faith and love are not feelings. Faith and love are decisions. Because of my love for you I believe in you. Believe in yourself. Continue to pray for one another. Continue to pray for those that are far away so that grace may fall upon grace upon them and that through your faithful prayers grace will open their heart and they too shall come to know the truth that will set them free.

10/18/12   (2 of 2)

    I will humble the proud. I will lift up the lowly. You see, all good things come from me. Apart from me you can do and bear no good. I came that you might have life and have it to the full. So you see, I who am, I who came into the world to redeem you, I who came to save you, remember, that's why they call me the

"Savior." So again I say I will humble the proud. I will raise up the lowly.

Do not worry so much about being leaders. Do not worry so much about what others think of you. Do not worry so much about the things of the world. Do not worry about popularity, for all who see me in you, all who see the works that you do in my name, that is witness enough, that should be all that is necessary for it is my work at work in all those who I raise up, all those that I call into service. Reflect my love. Reflect my healing power. Reflect my forgiveness and reflect my mercy. Be only concerned that you are decreasing and I am increasing within you.

11/8/12

The souls of the just are indeed in my hands, so do not worry, do not fear. You see, I have told you that I go before you and prepare a place for you so that where I am you shall also be. And indeed, those who have gone before you are experiencing love in its fullness, joy in its fullness. They have come through the fire of testing and rejoice in what they see and what they have heard. I wish you had ears to hear and eyes to see that I am not far from you.

I tell you this very day not to fear. I tell you, now in the present moment, be not afraid. Am I not your Lord, your Savior, your Redeemer? Am I not your all in all? Then why is your soul so downcast? Why are you afraid of the future? I told you that I would have a Remnant. I have prepared your hearts, your minds and your spirits to rejoice always. Indeed I say it again, rejoice always and pray unceasingly for those who do not know me, for those who lack faith, for those who have no hope except the hope they place in themselves, in their belongings. They have no idea that all things will pass away, but my word will never pass away. It is with my word that I bathe you, strengthen you, deliver you, heal you, and not only you but all those that you love, all those that you pray for.

I ask you now to give your all, all that you have. If you think you have a little bit of faith, give me all of it and I will multiply it. If you think you have just a little bit of wisdom, I will give you a double portion as you surrender it to me. Give me your trials, your tribulations, your fears, your anxieties, yes, even your doubts. Give them to me and in their place I will fill you with my Spirit. I will fill you with a spirit of boldness. I will fill you with courage, with grace upon grace. Do not look to the world for your peace for you will not find it there, but look to me for I am the Prince of peace, the King of peace. Look to me for I am the one who goes before you and prepares the way. Your ways are not my ways. My ways are so far above your ways.

So do not be dismayed. Again I tell you be not afraid. Fear is useless. What is needed is trust. Do not fear or worry about what can happen in this world. Do not worry about the situations and the circumstances that will come to pass. Only place your hope and your trust in me and know that I, your Lord, your God, hold you in the palm of my hand. Do not be afraid. I say it again, fear is useless. What is needed now is trust.

11/15/12

You are indeed, each of you, a soldier for Christ ... a term that seems old-fashioned, even insignificant today. The world has fallen so far from grace. I say to you, I say to each of you, to invoke, invoke the power of my name often. You see, I do lead you in battle by the power of my name, this is true. My name as I have said over and over again, my name and the power of my name, is indeed a shield. I surround you with a bastion of angels. You do not fight alone. Did I not tell you that the battle is mine, and I go before you, but I call you to be aware of the time. It is a time for battle and I place my angels, bastions of angels, around you and all those who are called by my name, and I speak to each of you and my word is to go out throughout all the ends of the earth. This word is not for you alone and you must do whatever you can do in your power to bring this truth to others. You will face much confusion ... great battles ... darkness ... confusion. You will be ready to give up on your own, but you see, you are not on your own. All mine who are called by my name I will bless, anoint, safeguard, empower, heal, strengthen in weakness, so that you will shine like a bright light in the darkness. This is a time you must remember that you are in a battle but you do not fight alone for the battle is mine and I am victor and you are not victims. I call you too to be victorious. I call you to remember that all the battles that you fight day in and day out on a personal level, you don't fight them alone either. You see, I am with you. I have come that you might have my life within you, my life flowing through you. You do not battle alone. I will rip down the strongholds in your life but you must be open to the power of my Spirit at work in you. You must decrease so that I might increase within you. This is how you will become a strong warrior. All those who belong to me put on your armor and remember that I am with you. Remember that my name is above every other name, every disaster, every tragedy. I am the Lord your God. There will be no other gods before me. This I say again, I alone am the Lord your God. You can only serve one God: Father, Son and Holy Spirit … Triune God.

      I tell you this night that you must invoke the power of a great warrior who fought a great battle. I call you to invoke St. Michael the archangel. Invoke him daily for he will go before you and fight. You do not see with eyes in the natural. You will see with eyes of faith and I call you to place all of your being at my disposal for you see, it will be you that will safeguard and carry my word in your heart. It is my word that will renew, restore, refresh, heal, bind-up … my word. All other things will pass away but I assure you my word will never pass. My word is ever new, ever ancient … like my Church, ever ancient yet ever new. Listen, be observant, be obedient to my one, holy, catholic and apostolic Church. Obedience, again, seen so often today as insignificant, out of date, a thing of the past. "I will not serve" is what I hear. But you, you come to serve me and I promise you

I will surround you with my angels. Again I say, invoke St. Michael my warrior. This is a time indeed, the time to be aware of the battle that you are in. A time to know that you do not need to fight for I will fight ... the battle is mine. And to all of you, you have nothing to fear for those who know me, those who follow me, those who seek me, those who implore my mercy, I will raise you up and you will be a light shining brightly in the darkness to lead others to safety.

This is indeed a time to listen to my vicar. This is indeed a time to be obedient. Though a remnant it may be, an obedient remnant it shall be. Anyone who does not adhere to the authority in the Church, anyone who does not humble themselves, you see, it is my authority, it is my authority in the Church because have I not said that through baptism and the renewal of the Holy Spirit, the Church will be safe-guarded. Be obedient. Rely not on your own understanding but know that I have left my Spirit to safeguard Mother Church. Know this, these words are true and they will be effective. Take them into your heart so that your light might shine brightly in the darkness.

11/29/12

Have you yet to understand the truth that every single action, every set of circumstances for your life there is a purpose and a plan, and these situations, these circumstances, take place in your life and you're not even aware that I work everything out for a greater good. You lament time and time again: Lord why have you left me, Lord where are you, Do you not see me struggling, Do you not see that I am weak and I need your strength? This is not just some of you. This cry goes out over all the earth. Why do my people not hear? Why do they not respond to my word? My word is living, it's effective, and yet they have ears and do not hear. They have eyes and they do not see. They will not listen. I have sent my word time and time again and they would rather put their hands over their ears so they can say I never knew, I never heard. So many have turned away from me within the Church and outside of the Church. They have decided that their ways are better than my ways and slowly but surely as they no longer are bathed in my word, slowly but surely they slipped out of the light and into the darkness.

      But you, it must be different with you. You must not only hear my word but act upon it. I call you to pray, to fast. I call you to really begin to run, run to my arms that await you to give you love and mercy and forgiveness through the sacramental life of the Church. My Church is being persecuted, but I tell you to stand firm for this is only the beginning. I tell you to believe with all your heart, your soul, your strength … believe in me. Believe in my word. My promises will be fulfilled, of this I assure you. Don't worry about anybody else's word being fulfilled for I am the greatest "promise keeper." When I promise, it shall come to pass. The Church will suffer much. Many priests will fall, but I will raise up many more in their place filled with holy boldness and courage and grace and strength to lead my people, my sheep, to cry out as the shepherd cries out himself. There will be much to take place, and again I would say to you these things must happen. Be not afraid. I call you to be at peace. This is a time of tribulation but also a time, again as I say, of great mercy. You are "mercy givers." Do you realize it? Have you come to understand that truth yet? You are called to be "Christ givers" for as I abide in you I seek you to go forth and allow others to come to me for they will see me living in you and they will come to believe.

You are my disciples and you hear my voice and you follow. So I say to you it is not by chance that you have come this night. It is indeed a divine appointment for I speak to your hearts and I tell you to be a people prepared, a people to be open for not only am I reaching out to draw others into my own heart but I have sent my Mother time and time and time again. Have you not noticed how urgently she comes? She calls to all the world, not to the areas alone that she appears in, but to all the world her message goes forth to pray, to fast.

And you, I call you to be steadfast for not only you but all those that you pray for, all those that you love. And all those who have gone before you are praying for you and those you love. Let not your heart be troubled and do not fear. This is a time, this is a time indeed for the light of Christ to shine brightly dispelling the darkness. Things will change but I am the same yesterday, today and forever. So allow me to move in you and through you. Allow me to guide you and lead you, and do not be concerned about anything that takes place for these things must happen. Know that I have a work for each of you to do and this is what you must focus on. So go indeed and make new disciples. This is a time of glory. This is a time of a great outpouring of my Spirit upon the earth ... divine mercy flowing, falling down, grace upon grace from the heavens for those who believe. And for those who do not believe I send you out to draw them back into the faith. My Church in the end will be a haven. So go and make disciples.

12/13/12

I would not have you store up riches. I would not have you store up material things. I want you to look to others. I want you to be able to help ... to help those who are in need. I want you to be aware of the many ways that I have blessed you abundantly. You have family and friends to love you and to comfort you, to walk along the journey with you when you are struggling, when you're upset, even when you fear or doubt. Yes, someone in your life that can bring you comfort, someone that can encourage you, someone who can give you peace of mind because these are the people that I have surrounded you with. These are the gifts that I have given you ... "angels" to accompany you on your journey.

But many, many are broken. Many are alone. Many are suffering heartache. Many are suffering rejection and the pain that is in their heart is great. They have no one to give them words of encouragement. They've wandered away from me so they have ears but do not hear and they have eyes but they do not see and their hearts have grown like stone. But you, you have been given much. But you see, do not take for granted what I have given you. What I give to you I give to you to share. If you have peace in your heart, so much peace that it overflows and people seek you out, that peace is my gift to you to give to others. If you have wisdom that others wear themselves out coming to your door, that is my gift, the gift of wisdom that I have given to you and so I call you to give to others that wisdom, that knowledge, that understanding. I could continue to go on but you know the meaning of these words. You are to give what you have received and give it in abundance, give it freely, give it out of love. You who have no time, still give your time. You who have no money, still give the little money that you have. To you much is given, I say it again, and much will be required of you.

   I would not have you grow weary nor tired on your journey. I would not have your hands idle. I would not have you waste away the day, but if you're still and you seek me I will come to you and I will busy your hands and your heart and your mind and your spirit on the things that I call you to do and the only way you'll know this is to take this quiet time, to take this stillness and to listen to me speak to you. I want to calm you. I want to strengthen you so that you can bring that calm, that peace, into a frantic world. I want to give you my love so you can love those who have gone astray, those who are judged, those who are distained. Those are the ones that I call you to pray for. They are the ones that I call you to be gentle with. They are the ones I call you to show them the light of my life within you. Do not grow weary of doing good for I fan the flame myself by the breath of my Spirit within you so that the fire of my love might burn away everything that is impure and fill you with a zeal and a passion and an enthusiasm that you know as sure as anything that it is me moving in you. Oh, I have given you much. Continue to remember the greatest "Gift-giver", the greatest "Promise-keeper", and then remind others so that they too can come and follow me.

12/20/12

You see, you are the heralds of the good news. It is my word you will speak and it is with my love that you will reach out to others in. It will be my compassion that warms hearts that have grown cold. You are called to bring good tidings to everywhere you go. You must not be concerned with those that would laugh at you, those that would not believe you, those that would even scoff at you and sneer ... yes, even those that would talk about you ... those that would lie and try to break down your witness. For you see, the work I send you to do to bring good tidings, good news into everyone's life that I send you into ... it is this, this truth that you must remember: you must always trust in my word. You must trust that if I call you to this mission that I will give you everything necessary to live and move and have your being in me. Again I say, you are to be the heralds of glad tidings, good news. With all the bad news in the world today the world is waiting, waiting for good news, good news that will not pass away so it must be my word because my word will never pass away.

I anoint you. I empower you. I give you wisdom. And so you know, you know in your heart of hearts that it is I who works in you and through you. So do not depend on yourself. Do not worry about what you will say or how you are to do something. If the work is mine then I will bring it forth. My promises are true. I am faithful. I do not change. I am the same yesterday, today and forever. I am the only one that you can put your hope in. I am the only one that you can trust. Others, though you love them, do not have the ability to meet each and every one of your needs, and surely not the desires of all that lies within your heart. Yes it is only I. I am … I am the good news. I am the one who sends you. I am the one who will hold all accountable. I am the one who will stand and plead your case. I ask only that you trust in my love, trust in my ways and rely not on your own understanding. If my word goes forth it will accomplish the work it is sent to do. Everywhere I send you, you bring my word. It dwells within you. You are indeed the temple of my Holy Spirit. My Spirit alone will sanctify you making you aware of Emmanuel, God with you.

You are never ever alone though you might not feel my presence, though you might question where am I in the midst of so many things that are going on in the world. Trust in my word that I will never leave you nor will I ever forsake you. Trust in my word that I am with you always even till the end of the age and trust in my word when I tell you that when I come again there will not be a need of any phone call, any message, any telegraph, any television. When I come again all will know, all will see. They will see the cross. They will see the glorious light shining down from the cross and then, then when I do come all will have had a time to turn to me for divine mercy. This is an hour of mercy. This is a time of great mercy. This is a time of joyful hope. You see, I will never leave you, ever leave you. Many will leave you. Many will disappoint you. Many in your family will break your heart. Many in your family will not adhere to the truth. But I give you this confident assurance this night: as you lift them to me I take them to my own heart and I draw them ever so tenderly to my own heart because you've remained faithful. It is grace at work. You are saved by grace through faith and all those that you pray for, all of them, will be saved too by your faith through grace.

(END OF VOLUME V)

Volume 6

Nihil Obstat
Rev. Msgr. Joseph G. Prior

Imprimatur
Archbishop Charles J. Chaput
Archiepiscopus Philadelphiensis
October 18, 2018

No portion of this book may be reproduced in any form without written permission from the Publisher:
Morning Star – New Dawn Ministries
P.O. Box 1446
Blue Bell, PA 19422
If unavailable in local bookstores, additional copies of this book may be purchased by writing to the Publisher at the above address.

Copyright, 2019 By Kathleen McCarthy
ALL RIGHTS RESERVED   ISBN 978-0-9641873-3-7

Artwork by Margaret M. Matt

1/3/13

Do you really believe that my name is above every other name? Do you believe that I am the way, the truth and the life? There is no other way that will lead you to eternal life. There is no other truth that will set you free. Do you really believe that my name is above every other name? Every sin that you could ever think of, every sin that you could ever experience, every addiction, every sickness, every illness ... my name is above them all. You must come to believe this truth so that in believing in the name of Jesus that every other name shall bend under the mighty weight of the Triune God. I need only send my word. But you ... do you really believe in the power of my name, the almighty power in the name of Jesus? You recited from scripture that every knee shall bow, every tongue profess that Jesus Christ is Lord, but if you really believed, if you really understood, then you would not loose your peace about the things that take place in your heart, in your world, in your families, in your businesses, in your livelihoods, in your missions. You would believe that I am the Lord God almighty, and so I just want to remind each of you that I not only hold each of you in the palm of my hand but I hold each and every one that you pray for ... all your children, all your family members, all your grandchildren. I ask you to remember that faith comes by hearing.

It is important that you share what I have done in your midst. It is important that you would share with others what I have done in your life so that as they hear this truth they too will begin to believe in the power of my love ... the power of my love that was able to take all the sins of the world to the cross so that you could be free, free to be all that I call you to be. My name is indeed above every other name. My name protects you. Do you realize it? My name actually protects you. When you are in the midst of a bout of fear or anxieties or in times of doubt or confusion, times when you are so troubled you can not pray ... yes, I understand, and that's why I tell you that only utter the name, my name, the name of Jesus, and all the strongholds in your life, all those things that would rob you of peace, those chains will drop, the strongholds will be torn down when you realize that I am the Lord your God almighty and that my name is above every other name.

So be at peace. Offer me your wounds, your fears, your doubts, your anxieties ... offer me your families, offer me all that you are so that I can bless you to become all that I call you to be.

1/31/13 (1 of 2)

You see, there is always a place for each of you to go and that's to reach out because I am within your brothers, your sisters, your mothers and your fathers but I am, most importantly, I'm in each and every one of you. Many times you feel that you are unloved. You feel that you've never really been appreciated. You feel that you've been taken for granted time and time again. You've been used and abused. You've been rejected. You've been lonely. And yet at other times you are aware of many of the blessings that are in your life. However, you forget to acknowledge that those blessings ... they are from my heart to your heart. They come from my life to your lives.

    I have loved each and every one of you. I have called each and every one of you by name. Do you know that I have left my word to remind you that before you were even in your mother's womb I knew you? Yes, before you were even in your mother's womb you were in my heart. I fashioned you. I molded you. I transformed you into all that I've called you to be. You have failed to reach that potential yet, but I still call and I wait for your response day in and day out. I wait. I wait till you feel there's nowhere else to go and you'll try turning to me and then I tenderly hold you close to my own heart. I ask my mother to place her mantle over you drawing you deeper and deeper into the Spirit of my own love for you. And then after awhile, sure enough, you drift away again when you experience the joy that I've placed within you, the joy that can well up and dispel those dark times, the loneliness, the brokenness, the lack of gratitude and appreciation from others. And then once again when your heart aches, when you feel alone, you turn again to me.

    But you see, I want you to know, I want you to know without any inner doubts that I have a plan for your life and that there's a great purpose and that purpose is deep within you, and I want you to experience the purpose that I have given you to be a light shining brightly in the darkness. There is a time coming when darkness will spread over the earth quicker than you could ever imagine and that's why your light must shine brightly so that others would find their way to me seeing my light shine through you. You will be the gift. You will be the gift of my love and my presence and my mercy and my forgiveness on the earth. So I call you to be vigilant. I call you to remember that every day is a new beginning. I call you to remember that I am with you always. I walk along with you, aside of you. I well up within you. I call to you from afar and I hold you close when you come to me. When, my child, will you begin to realize that I have a purpose and plan for your life? One that will leave you feeling that you are who you were created to be ... my child. I have so much I want you to experience, so much I want you to yet do, so much that I want you to give to others that I bring into your life. Please don't wait so long to turn to me because you could have this peace at every moment, every day, because it is the power of my Holy Spirit, the power of my life, my authority, within you that will indeed give you a peace that the world will never rob you of.

1/31/13 (2 of 2)

I am calling all of my people together. I am calling my children, children of the most high God. I am calling them. I am drawing them through the power of my Holy Spirit working in them and through them. Remember this and never forget it: Mary in the fullness of time was set aside to give her very flesh and blood to my son, Jesus. She is indeed the spouse of my Holy

Spirit and the two, have I not told you even in the natural, shall become one. I send my Spirit into the world to draw my people together. And Mary, mother of Jesus, her son, is mother of all and she intercedes to her son, Jesus, for all of you, for all of her children. And so I would remind you to remember and not to forget: if Jesus, the savior of the world, is her son, are not you, Jesus' brothers and sisters, also her children? When the world begins to understand this truth, swiftly they all will come together, all of them will come to give praise and honor and glory to the one Triune God and honor to the Mother who is chosen to be the vessel that salvation should come through. So I tell you this night, make no mistake, I have called and will call ... I will call all my children together. There will be one shepherd and one flock, of this you can be sure. Again I will say, I am calling my people together. There will be one shepherd and one flock.

2/7/13

I want you to ponder in your heart and in your mind this truth: all of you, each of you, are like a book, living, walking and moving, in this time, in this place. You are the book of your life, and chapter by chapter you have lived life, and so I say to you that this book of your life must be read by others so that they can see in you how you have experienced the living God. They must see in you how you have, not only grown, but more importantly, how you've fallen more and more in love because you know how much your God is in love with you. And this is what will touch other people's hearts. This is the story that the world relates to: your personal journey.

And each chapter where you have suffered, where you have been filled with joy, times of darkness where my light had dispelled it ... these are the stories that move people's hearts. So your life must be a story about the infinite love that I have for each one of you. It must be a story about my mercy that I have shown each of you time and time again. It must be a story where you were deeply disturbed with anxieties and fears and doubts and how the gift of my wisdom, my knowledge, my grace and strength filled you with confident assurance.

And they might read it as a book. This is your journey, your life, and so I say to you ponder the thought that each of you are a book that other people will read and so I call you to be credible in all things. I call you to walk in confident assurance. I call you to live out your faith that it might be a light to others, that it might be a sign of hope to others because it is that authentic witness that I call you to be that will impact your life and will make a statement in the hearts of those who are seeking truth.

So it is not so much by your words, it is how authentically you live out your faith. Even in the midst of trials and tribulations, people will be astounded at your peace and they will know it comes from somebody greater than yourself. It comes from the God who loves you in the midst of trials and struggles, fears and doubt, the God who loves you and breaks the bonds of addictions to set you free. Your authenticity will make the difference in the world. When your words and actions line up in life, chapter by chapter that changes constantly, so that all who look and see you would surely exclaim this is truth, this life that they look at, they would surely say, it is the Lord.

So I call you to ponder. I call you to act upon this word. I call you to realize that others are watching and when they see me living in you, when they see an authentic witness of a Christian life, then they too will hunger and thirst for righteousness' sake as their lives take on another chapter in their book of life.

2/21/13

You see, the joy of the Lord is your strength. This is not mere words, it's not a nice saying, it's a truth. Even in the most sorrowful circumstances, even in times of hardship, even in times of difficult circumstances … my joy is your strength. The joy of the Lord is your strength. When you can not yield to joy in the midst of trials and tribulations then you are depending on your strength. But I tell you my joy is your strength … such a simple exclamation for power and strength, such a simple explanation of the joy of the Lord.

I call each of you to be luminaries. Yes, luminaries because I fill you with my light and it is my light that I call you to share with others so that they can see in you my joy. When they look at you and see all that's going on in the world, in your lives, in their lives, and they see you at peace, they see you experiencing a joy that goes beyond yourself, they know it is me living in you. Luminaries bringing the light of Christ out into the darkness to dispel the darkness.

I have sent word after word, news flash after news flash, urgency, time and time again, and yet so often my Church has been asleep. I tell you this: in these times of uncertainty, in these times of darkness, I assure you I will never leave nor forsake you. Mother Church will reign regardless of who would try to quiet her down, shut her up, for my word is living and it is effective. My presence alive, my life living, my heart beating, my body complete and whole, mind, body, spirit, living in every tabernacle all over the world. This light must shine in the darkness, and you must bring my light out into the world.

Do not be afraid of ridicule. Do not let your pride stand in the way of speaking the truth where a soul could be set free. Pray to me. Pray to the Holy Spirit for wisdom and knowledge and grace and strength for this journey that you are on. You see, I've given you life in this time, in this place, because it is you that I have called by name. It is you that I have chosen. It is you that I send. I have sent news flashes and urgent messages to wake up the Church. I ask you to remain vigilant, not to be caught sleeping, but be vigilant and aware of all that is taking place. This is indeed a pivotal time in the Church. This is an urgent time in the Church. Mother Church will be a place of security. She will be a sanctuary, and yet so many will come against her, but the gates of hell will not prevail. I will lead my people and I will bring light to dispel the darkness and my light abides in each of you.

So do not be afraid. Allow my joy to be your strength, for I send you out, I send you out to do a mighty work in an urgent time. This is a time, again I tell you, of divine mercy. This is a time I call you to wrap your children in the rosary. I call you to remember this: be not afraid. Let not your heart be troubled, for you know the truth. This truth must be taken out to others in your lives, in your families, in your workplaces, so that many who would be lost would be saved through bringing truth, my truth, that can set them free.

3/7/13

I call each and every one of you to surrender. I ask you to really allow me to be Lord over your life. Oh, I know you think that your way is the best way. I know you think that it's your life and nobody knows it better than you, so you can make those decisions, you can act on all the ways that you feel that you should go, however, I tell you now, it is I living in you and through you that will lead you to walk on the path that I have chosen for you. You see, I know you better than you know yourself. Was it not I who formed you? Was it not I who conceived you in my own mind and in my own heart? Was it not I that called you forth into the world? I say to you now, even though you think that your ways are better, that your will is best, I tell you there could be nothing further from the truth. You see, I want to mold you and transform you into all that I call you to be. I want to fill you with power, the power that comes from my Spirit at work in your life. I want to fill your heart and your mind and your spirit with knowledge so you will not perish. You know I have said it, it has been written: "my people perish for lack of knowledge." And so I want to give you wisdom and knowledge and grace upon grace and to do so I need you to invite me in to all the areas of your life, not some of the parts, not ask me to come into your heart and stifle me from trying to heal and renew and restore. I want to break down walls that you have put up through the years, walls that have really entrapped you. You've built them to keep others out, however, this turned out that you are the one trapped inside the walls, and so I am blowing the trumpet and the walls are coming down. It is I, I myself, who am molding and transforming. I need your "yes." I need your surrender. I will not force myself upon you. I knock at your door and I ask you to open it. And you are living out your life in all these different relationships and all the busyness of the world, but you see, I want to lead you to where I want you to go and I want to stop you from going places that you want to go, for I know the plans I have for you. My plans will bring you prosperity. I want to heal you. I want you to have your hope in me because when you place your hope in me, you will have the courage you need.

      These are times of great tribulation and yet you fail to recognize, time and time again, that I've sent my word. Time and time again, my word has proclaimed the truth that will set my people free. I tell you over and over and over again that it is you that will bring the good news out into the world. There is an urgency, I say it again. I need you to focus on me. I need you to trust in my great deep love for each and every one of you, and not only you, but all those that you love ... for your mates, your siblings, all of those that I place in your care, all those that I put in your life, those that are not easy to love, those that often bring you to a point of frustration and struggle. These are the people I bring into your life that you might grow more fully in love, in compassion, in mercy, in grace and strength, and when you realize this you will recognize that I have formed you and reformed you time and time again more perfectly into my own image and likeness.

These are indeed the days of Elijah. These are indeed times of great mercy and light. What are you going to do? Are you willing to go forth? Are you willing to focus on me and not your problems, for as you keep your eyes on me, as you place your focus on me, I assure you I will work in all of your problems. I will take you through the valley. I will not leave you alone nor orphan you. I have paid a great price for each and every one of you, and so I ask you this night to go in my name. I ask you this night to speak my truth, be my ambassadors whether it's convenient or inconvenient. I ask you to decrease so that I might increase within you. I ask you to continue to pray. The prayers of righteous people are powerful indeed. And as you minister to those who know me not, you yourself will receive healing upon healing.

So go therefore and make disciples for I would again have not one soul lost.

3/14/13   *(Pope Francis was just elected.)*

    Now indeed it begins. It begins indeed. I have called, I have called my son and he has answered "Here I am." Now is the time, and now is the hour for him to guide and lead with Our Lady, my Holy Mother, that I gave to each one of you on one side and my Eucharistic Heart, beating, my heart flowing out with grace upon grace of divine mercy, on the other side. This in indeed the hour and the time that I have raised up my son. Under great stress and turmoil and great challenges he will lead my people into the turmoils of the raging seas and the horrific winds. He will be the healing balm that will bring my peace, the healing balm from Gilead. This is what he will bring to the world. And for all those who have turned away and for all those who have lost faith, for all those who have turned to darkness and for all those who have said that God is not alive, that He does not exist, I solemnly assure you they will know. They will come to see and understand. They will come to their senses through these times, through these times of great challenge and struggle. They will come to their senses. Their minds and hearts will truly be enlightened. This is a time of great hope. This is a time of great joy. Let your hearts rejoice. Lift up your hands and praise my Holy name. Let not your hearts be troubled. This is a time that was meant to be and my son shall guide and lead through these stormy waters and you shall see … they shall come home. They shall come back to their faith. They shall come home to the Church that I instituted myself. A remnant though it be, it'll be one that will renew the face of the earth.

3/21/13

My people have been lulled to sleep. My heart aches and so I wish that all my people who know me and love me and serve me would go forth with a new zeal, with a new passion, one that you have not yet experienced, for I've taken you to a new glory. Did I not tell you that I would take you from glory to glory? And so as you place your hope and your trust in me, I will raise you to another glory. I will enlighten your mind and your hearts and your understanding in the spirit to new truth. I await you to give me your "Yes." I await your invitation to come in and move in you and through you powerfully. My people indeed have been lulled to sleep and they will awaken I assure you. They will be awakened by all the things that shall come about to wake up this world and, in particular, for the United States of America. It is a time that the light, my light, must shine like a beacon piercing the darkness. This is a time. It is a time to teach my people. It is a time to speak my word, bring forth my healing, and above all, bring the truth that will set my people free. For you see, when they do wake up, they will be a people in frenzy. They will be confused. They will doubt. They will have lost hope and they've lost hope because they have never placed their hope in me. They have placed their hope in things, in people, in places.

But you see, it is you and those who believe, really believe in me, those who have come to know me, those who have come to love the truth of our one holy, catholic and apostolic Church, the Church that I myself instituted, and the gates of hell will indeed try to come against this

Church, but it'll be the people who remain faithful and true that will take my peace that goes beyond all understanding, that will be able to bring my peace to the world ... my peace to dispel the fear, the anxiety, the darkness and the doubt and the hopelessness that will be in the world. But you, I send you and I bring others to you so that they might hear the truth and they will be set free. Their fears, their anxieties, their hopelessness, their frustrations ... you see, they're all in vain. It is when they come to believe that I am a God of love and mercy, a God who will never leave them nor forsake them, it is then and then alone that they will be snatched free from the path of destruction. It will be then and only then when they will be able to receive the power of grace that is at work in the world through you. They will be drawn back and they, once again as I have been reminding you, will come back to the security of the Church where they will indeed eat my body and drink my blood, where they will indeed come to recognize me in the breaking of the bread, when they will come to believe without any doubt that I am alive and that my heart is beating in every tabernacle all over the world. And when they come to know this truth, the churches once again will be alive with zeal and passion and hope, for those who place their hope in me will never be put to shame. Those who place their hope and trust in me will never be disappointed.

4/4/13

I speak my word that it might take root in your heart and in your mind and in your spirit. You see, the word that I give you is a living word, is a word that brings transformation, power and healing. Justice and mercy came together on the cross. You see, because you have placed your hope and your trust in me, justice is made clear for I paid the price for the sins of the world. And it was mercy, my mercy, mercy from above, that flowed out of my side ... water and blood ... mercy for the whole world.

And so I say to you, I say to you right now, you do not understand my ways. Many times you are confused and wonder where I am in the midst of these trials and circumstances. You wonder why I am not entering into your pain and your suffering. You wonder where I am when tragedy strikes, and in brokenness you can not feel me and so you think I am not present. Nothing could be further from the truth. I am the truth and my ways, again, are so far above your ways, but my ways are right, just, and yes, even though you do not have eyes to see or a mind to comprehend, my ways are just and full of mercy. I am concerned for every soul, every soul, and so my way, because I am outside of time and space, I see all and I know all, and so I tell you that the closer you come to know me and to love me and to serve me, you will begin to understand that I am indeed a God of mercy and love and you will come to trust in me more and more each day. You see, I have come into the world to give you not only peace, to give you not only my joy, but I come to give you hope, a hope that will never disappoint and so I ask you this very moment to believe that I am present even when you feel me not, that I am present in the midst of everything that is going on in your life and the lives of those that you love. Often times, my sons and daughters, the very things that you are angry and anxious about are the very things that I am working together for a greater good. And so you loose your peace because I do not respond to your way. I do not respond to working your situation or your circumstance or your problems out to your liking. But as you come to know me and love me and serve me more fully, as you enter out into the deep, you will surely come to understand that in all these things justice and mercy meet for the greater good of not only your soul but the souls of those that you love, the souls of the just and the unjust, the souls that you worry about, the souls that you pray for, the souls that you believe are lost.

You see, your trust is the greatest gift you offer me. It's like incense flowing up surrounding my heart. Incense ... that is what your trust is to me. And so I say now, know that whatever is going on I am working it together not just for good but for a greater good for I have loved you with a love that goes beyond all understanding. I did it for you my people. I went to the cross for you. It was because of you and my love for you that I laid down my life that you might have my life and have it to the full.

4/11/13

I have called each of you by name. I have called you from the midst of turmoil and the midst of impatience. I have called you in the midst of anxiety and fear. I have called you in the midst of your curiosity. I have called you in the midst of your daily living. I've called you to tell you that I'm doing a new thing in your life … yes, in your life. I have sent my word. The word I sent has gone forth and it will not return void. I have called you and you have responded to my call. You see, I am doing something new, something new in your life, and my heart rejoices because you came questioning, but you came. You have an open mind and an open heart and an open spirit.

Oh yes, you have many questions and many concerns, but I tell you that you are my own. I tell you that I have fashioned you and molded you into the very person that I call you to be. There are no accidents. I have a great plan for your life. You were created with a purpose … for my purpose. And because of this I will reveal myself more and more to you, and I will reveal myself more and more to you through the breaking of the bread for as you eat my body and drink my blood you will be strengthened. You will be filled with grace and courage and strength and holy boldness, for these times are tumultuous to say the least.

But you see I am sending out my healing love. I am sending out my word through new disciples. You are those disciples. I have hidden my word in your heart for this perfect timing. You see, I wait and I call to you and then when you open your heart and ears to receive my word, to receive my call, it is then that I come in ... in power, in mercy, in love, in forgiveness, in healing. I have not only called you to save you, I have not only called you to my own heart for you, not only you but your whole household. So do not fear, this new work that I will do in you will give you a peace that will go beyond all understanding. When men put their hope and their trust in the things of the world, the things that give them temporary highs and temporary feelings of joy and temporary feelings of happiness, you see, my word that I speak to your hearts is not external ... it's internal, and this peace that I will give to you is a peace that you have not experienced so far and it's for this time that I have called you for there are many, many that need to be called too, and then many who need to hear the word of God and to see the fire of my love radiating out of you. Yes, I've called you, each one of you, with all your faults and all your weaknesses. It is in this weakness that others shall recognize me in the new work I will begin in you. They will look and they will know there is something different. You will be a contradiction to the world not so much by what you say but how you live. It is this witness that will draw many back to the Church, draw many back to my own heart. I wait, and I wait for you to come in expectant faith for the work I'm about to do in your midst. Oh, I have called you here by name and I will do a mighty work in your life.

Call to me. Ask me to fill you with my Spirit. I will fill you. I will renew you and I will give you a gift, the gift of repentance, that you might receive a joy that goes beyond all understanding. You are mine. You will be my hands and my feet and a voice bringing my words to all who need to hear because faith comes by hearing.

4/11/13   (2 of 2)

Let your ears be attuned. Let your ears be open to hear and your heart be willing to receive. There will be much turmoil. Many will rise up against the Church. I tell you this, this night, that you might understand that in the midst of turmoil, of all those that will come to attack the Church, this is a time of great mercy and grace. You must remain firm in your faith. For all those who have walked away, all those who refuse to believe, all those who have left to go to other churches ... they do not know the truth and the fullness of this truth and they have turned away not realizing that it is only through the power of my love and the Church that I instituted that they will be saved. They are being deceived and so I say to you this is a time of great mercy upon the earth.

I send you out to bring the truth to set other people free. For all those who will remain in me, they will be victorious. For all those who place their hope and trust in my shepherd, even in the midst of confusion and doubt, I tell you to stand firm for I will lead the Church through tumultuous times. I will lead the Church through my shepherd who I have called. You must eat my body and drink my blood for it is in my Eucharistic Presence that I will embolden you, that I will strengthen you, that I fill you with grace beyond all understanding. I say this so that your hearts will not be troubled but that you will know that these things will come to pass.

Pray for my shepherds. Pray for your priests for many will wander off and fall away, but I assure you I am raising up new shepherds. I assure you I am filling those who have remained faithful with wisdom and knowledge and understanding and holy boldness, and then with them standing steadfast with the Holy Father, I myself will come to defend my Church. So be not afraid but seize this time of grace and mercy. Go out into the world and draw others to my Sacred Heart. Draw them through the rosary. Through my mother's mantel her prayers will watch over and protect. Through the rosary, just like of old, Our Lady will be victorious. Trust in my word and do not believe in the words of the world.

4/18/13 (1 of 2)

For all of you and for all those who seek me, for all of those who open their hearts and their minds and their spirits and invite me in, I tell you I indeed have come to heal my Mystical Body. I have come as a liberator to set my people free. I have come as a lover to love you into wholeness in the midst of your brokenness, in your pain, in your insecurities and your fears and your anxieties. I have come that you might have life and have it to the full. Have I not told you this? And so indeed I do come and I am within you, and a bastion of angels surrounds you as well as all of those who have run the good race and fought the good fight. They are constantly around you as a cloud of witnesses encouraging you on to be that witness, the witness of the life of Christ that dwells within you.

You see, I gather you into my own arms. So often throughout the day I embrace you. I hold you close to my own heart. I speak tenderly to you. I fill your days often with surprises. I give you my joy so that your joy might be complete. And in a 24 hour period a very few people recognize those visits, but you seek me with a sincere heart. I will put my hand over each and every one of you. I will protect you and I will go before you and prepare the way in which I want each of you to walk. I want to fill you with wisdom and knowledge and grace. I want you to know that in my arms, held against my Sacred Heart, I will fill you with love, light and grace. And for all of those who have wandered off ... even you, you see, I've called you that you would come back to me. And deep within your heart and soul you knew it was I calling, and finally you surrendered, finally you acted and you came, and now I tell you because of your faith, because of your openness, because of trusting me a little bit more each day I will do a work deep within your heart and your soul. I will give you a peace that the world will no longer be able to rob you of. I have much, much for you to do. I have much to give to you. So place your hope and trust in me for I gather my people in my arms and I go after all those who have walked away and I send you out to bring truth and the love of God to all those so that none would be lost.

4/18/13 (2 of 2)

I remind you to stand fast in your faith. I say it again, stand faithfully, stand strong in your faith. Although many people are leaving the Church, the Church that I shed my very blood for, they are walking away and they're scattered in so many other places now, but I tell you, you must remain in faith in your one, holy, catholic and apostolic Church. I will take care of my own. I will watch over and protect and bless and anoint all those who place their hope and their trust in me. This again I tell you is a time of divine mercy and you see, it is in faithful men and women like yourself, even amidst trepidation, it'll be through men and women like you who have stood fast and stood tall in the face of adversity and trials and tribulations. You will be safe and secure for I will hide you in my own heart.

You have a work to do. You have a work that has been anointed and blessed. You have indeed been created for a purpose and I have created you with a purpose. You have not even begun to understand all the wonderful ways that I will bless you, take care of you, and work all things together for good in your lives. You have not even begun to understand nor comprehend what I am in the midst of doing for you, but I will reveal more and more. You see, as you eat my body and drink my blood you will grow more and more aware of what I would have you do. As you eat my body and drink my blood you will be safeguarded from all the evil. Come closer and closer for your safety, your peace, your joy is in me.

5/2/13

I remind you to call on the power of my Spirit. I left you the Paraclete. I left you my Spirit, the Spirit of God that dwells in you, God Himself is within you, and you have been gifted. I want you to begin to call on the power of the Holy Spirit. You see, it is only through the working and the power of the Holy Spirit working in you and through you that you can touch other people's lives, that your words will have a dramatic effect on other people's lives, that your healing touch would have an effect on other people's lives. I say to you that as the Father has loved me, so too He loves each of you. Imagine that! As He loves me ... as He loves me, He loves you! And as He has sent me, He too sends you. He sends you out into a world that is in such darkness. He sends you out with the good news to speak louder than all the bad news of the world.

So pray. Pray in all the big things and the little things of your daily life. Pray when you're lost, pray when you're confused, pray to my Spirit when you are upset or frightened. Pray to my Spirit when you feel depression coming on. My spirit abides within each one of you, and my Spirit wells up within you. My Spirit is moving in a powerful way. I am pouring out my Spirit. The power of my love is coming forth like nothing this world has ever experienced ... the fire of my love. Do not look at the dark. Do not look at all the world who continues to walk in darkness but look within. Yes, within, for the kingdom of God is within you. Never forget it. You're never ever alone, I'm always within you. When you confess me as Lord, when you follow my Commandments, when you live in me, I am always there.

I tell you I am lighting a fire on the earth. It will go like a wildfire. It will ignite the coldest hearts. It will warm the coldest hearts and melt them. How so you might say with a world that is so full of darkness, in a world that is so far removed from what I have called my people to be? How so, indeed? It is by the fire of my love, the fire that I am setting on the earth. You will see. You will be amazed. This is what has been told. A fire on the earth that indeed will spread throughout the world. It'll start with a little spark until it becomes a wildfire.

I am calling my people back to the Church. This is an absolute. Do not doubt. It'll come to pass. It must begin with you. It must begin with your "yes", and then I'll do the rest.

5/9/13

I call you to stay close, to stay close to my mother … my mother and your mother. You see, is she not Mother Church? Has she not been the very flesh and blood from whence I came and took on my own flesh and blood, my own humanity? So if she is my mother and I have instituted the one, holy, catholic and apostolic Church, then it is only fitting that she is mother of the Church as well. Follow her. Follow her example for she loves as a mother loves. She places your petitions, when they come through her, right before my own sacred heart, the heart that I told you is in love with you. Nobody knows the Son like the Father and the mother. Just like you know your children ... nobody knows them as well as you do ... so too it is with my mother, with my Father. My mother said "yes" in the most trying and difficult of circumstances. She said "yes", and with her "yes" she brought me into the world. She brought me into the world to die so that each one of you might live. That's a mother's love, a love that trusted in the Father's love, a mother's love that knew always and forever that all things were possible with God. And if God would call her Son to Himself then she surely knew to trust in that, and so she did.

She's my mother and your mother and so I call you to be nurtured, nurtured by the sacramental life of the Church. I gave my flesh and my blood that you might receive that nourishment. I breathed on my apostles that you might receive forgiveness, unconditional forgiveness that, again, through the priest I might love you into wholeness. There is no sin so great that my mercy will not make the blackest of sin as white as the snow. This is a great message that must go out to the world. They must see my love, my forgiveness and my mercy through you.

How do they know God who they do not see? How do they begin to think about God who they do not see? How do they begin to love God they do not see? It is through you, through my Mystical Body, for I am God, there is no other god beside me. And because of this, others will receive from you a demonstration of my love. Love the unlovable, forgive the unforgivable, be-friend the stranger and bless those who do my work and I will bless you in abundance. Again, in you they will see me and when they see me and my love for them they will come and follow me.

5/16/13

Do not think for one moment ... no, not even for a moment, that you have come because you have decided to come to sit in my presence, that you have decided to come and look into this prayer community. You see, it was I, I am always calling to my people and you heard my call, you heard me whisper deep within your soul. And see, it's a grace because it was I first calling you, and you responded to this call. It is for me to prepare your hearts, your mind and your spirit. For you see, not only for you, but there will be others that will not even know or experience what you have but will be touched through you. This was a gift, a gift of my Spirit to you. It was me speaking in your heart, whispering to come and see and you came and you saw and now you have tasted the goodness of the Lord. There is no problem that can beset you that I will not work together for a greater good. There is no heartache that I will not assuage your heart and heal the wounds that are there. I know each and every one of them. I know the very source and the cause of those wounds and I have brought you that you might receive healing. And through these times of praise and coming together, I will set other people free through you ... those from your past that you have held bound that have wounded your heart and yes, even crushed your spirit at times. I am going to set them free through you so they will no longer have any power over you. It will be through you surrendering that hurt, that wound of the heart, the feelings of anger that still come when you think of them, the hurts that they caused and the damage that was done.

But you see, you are mine ... you are mine, and because you are mine I will minister to your own heart and to your own soul. I will set you free so that you become more and more of what I've called you to be before you were even in your mother's womb. You will know to love as I love, you will begin to forgive as I have forgiven you ... unconditionally. And as your heart begins to swell with the love that I have for you, a love that you really can not comprehend nor fully grasp, but you will begin to know that I am loving you into wholeness. The holes that have been in your heart will be filled with the gift of my Spirit bringing peace and grace and strength and freedom. I have loved you and you will begin to understand and experience my love more and more each day. I have called you by name. You are mine, and because you are mine, flesh of my flesh and bone of my bone, you will begin to take on my image and my likeness more perfectly. I see your attempts. I see your hope. I see your struggles. I see your pain. I see those moments of joy but you see, I have come that your joy would be complete. I have come to give you grace, to take you from grief to grace, to take you from darkness to light, to take you from emptiness and despair into the fullness of joy and hope.

You have only just begun, and you and I together, you and I walking together, talking together, sharing with one another ... you sharing your desires of your heart, your questions ... and me giving you my love, my wisdom, my knowledge and my understanding. I will touch many through you. It is a blessing and a gift that you have responded to the whisper of my call in your soul.

5/23/13   (1 of 2)

There is much darkness and evil in the world and yet people focus on and fear the dark when they need not. For did I not tell you because I am the light of the world, that you too, I send you out as the light. I send you out to dispel the darkness in other's lives. I send you out to bring the light that can dispel all the evil that you come in contact with. You see, others who fear the dark, they fear in vain. They should be focusing on the light. They should be focusing on the God who created them, on the Son who has redeemed them, and on the Spirit, the love between my Father and myself.

You see, it is through the Spirit that will bring unity in the body of Christ. And so though many would try to come against Christianity, though many would stand with their lies and their blasphemes, it is you that I call to dispel it with my light shining through you. It is my word that is truth. It is my word that will go forth and do the work I send it to do, and so this is what you must trust in. You must trust in my love. I do not ever act on my own. I act in you. Through my Spirit I work through you. My Father has commissioned not only me but He has commissioned each one of you, and He has commissioned you to go out and to be my ambassadors. He has commissioned you to preach the truth whether it's convenient or not. Now the world would seek to rob you of that truth and the evil and the darkness would try to distort it, but you must remain in me. You must always remember who you belong to, who you were created by, who called you into being, who sends you forth. It is the Father who has loved me. It is the Father who sends me and in turn you are sent. Do not forget that you belong to me. I paid a great price for you. It cost me everything, and yet how often do you even consider that fact?

  You fear often times the evil that is in the world when in truth you should be aware of my power, my might, my love. You should be aware that all things were created by me and so I tell you now, do not waste idle time worrying about what could happen, what if this happens. What you must do is remain in me that I might remain in you, and through the power and fire of my Spirit at work in you, hearts will be set on fire, darkness will be dispelled and unity, the unity of my Spirit, will draw others to be one in me by my power working through all those who are mine.

5/23/13 (2 of 2)

  Pray for the Holy Father. He will suffer much but I assure you that your prayers are like incense. This incense reaches the heavens and the light and love of my Spirit will come down and enfold him in the arms of my mother. Pray for the holy father for many, many in the world, in the Church, will come against him. He is not their idea of what they wanted but I have hand-picked him and he is my vicar. All those who are in awe of the work of my Spirit flowing out of him know this truth. I tell you to pray for the holy father and my princes of the Church that they might remain faithful. Your prayers are needed. Intercede, intercede for my Church and intercede for the holy father and the princes of the Church and all priests that they might shepherd my people. In times of persecution they will be able to bring peace and guidance. So intercede for the shepherds of my one, holy, catholic and apostolic Church. I have raised up holy men so that they might shepherd a holy people by the power of my Holy Spirit. And by the grace of my Father, in my name go forth. In my name and my name alone, rejoice.

5/30/13

I would not have my people going out into the world trying to fill their hunger, their thirst with the lies and the deceit of the world. You see, I have nourished each of you with my own body and my own blood. I continue to inebriate each of you in the blood that I have shed on the cross for you. And so I tell you to go and feed those who are hungry and thirsting, who would seek to listen to others as they are led to feed here or drink there. That is a nourishment that will destroy them and so I say to you, you nourish them, you feed them, so that they might come back to me. You feed them on my word spoken from the depth of your hearts. Feed them with the truth, my truth that abides in each and every one of you … my truth that will set everyone free. For as others try to satisfy the hunger and the need and the thirst by the things of the world they will be only satiated temporarily. But you see, my life will truly nourish them and transform them with the healing power of my love taking them from darkness and drawing them into the light, taking them from brokenness and receiving wholeness in me. So I say to you take my word, the word that dwells within you and take it out to those who are hungry and thirsty and who are in need. It is in this that others will see the transforming power of my love. And so as you eat my body and drink my blood, as you become what you receive, so too you will be able to take this to others, this new life, this transforming power of my Holy Spirit, this living word that dwells within you … the living word of God. By the Father who has created you, this is the mission that I call you to … a mission that will change the world, a mission that will bring new life, freedom and wholeness. This is what the world needs. The world needs each of you to sow the seeds of faith. Do not worry about where it lands for I will move in and through each and every person that the seed falls on. I will water. I will nourish. I will till the soils of their souls so that they will come back to me and they too will cry "my Lord and my God."

6/27/13 (1 of 2)

My people, I call you to be vigilant. I call you to stand firm in your faith, for again, the gates of hell continue to try to rip down the very Church that was instituted by me, myself. The very Church that was instituted by God the Father, by the Spirit of God, the very love between the Father and the Son, that very love I have poured out into each of your hearts. I have given you a spirit of boldness. I'm pouring out tonight courage. You must be vigilant. Your hearts must remain vigilant and no matter what takes place remember and never forget, this is my Church and though darkness falls upon and around her at times, my light will dispel the darkness.

I would not have my people scatter, I would not have my people scandalized. I would remind you again of the sanctity of life. I would remind you again of the sanctity of marriage between a man and a woman. I would remind you again that you are to be a voice crying out the truth that will set my people free. Slander will come. I speak to your hearts this night that you would be able to stand firm and be a voice of truth and strength and calm. I have spoken that your hearts would not be troubled, that you might have my peace, for the light will always overcome darkness. So be of sound mind. Be of one heart, one mind and one spirit. Defend the great pearl of great price, be ever ready to defend your faith. Be ever ready to stand vigilant, firm, because you know the truth and it will be the truth that will set others free. You know that I created one catholic Church. You know the marks of the Church. It is "one." You know it is "holy." It is "universal." It has been passed down through "apostolic" succession to this very day. This is the truth you must hold on to. Do not be scandalized by the sin of others. Do not be ashamed and do not hang your head low for although darkness will once again come against the Church, there are those that I have filled with holy boldness, with courage and valor who will not bend under pressure but who will remain a faithful voice. A voice crying out preparing the way of the Lord. A voice crying out guiding and directing and leading my sheep. I tell you this, that your hearts must not be troubled or afraid. I tell you to be at peace. I tell you to be vigilant and speak the truth whether it's in season or out of season. When you feel that maybe no one will listen, speak anyway. Love your brothers and sisters enough to speak the truth!

Remember: I lead you, I walk with you, my Spirit is within you, I watch over you, I protect you, I guide you. I go before you to prepare the way, you need only follow me. My mother's heart is always vigilant. Your heart must be vigilant too for all those souls, for your own, for your mates, for your children. Fear not, the joy of the Lord will be your strength.

6/27/13   (2 of 2)

In these days of unbelief, in these days of whitewash, whitewash of the truth, in these days where people use the language and twist it and turn it to present it as something good, something wholesome, you who know the truth know it's evil. Many of the princes of the Church will fall. You must never look to man as being all good and deserving of all of your love. You must only look to God who is all and is all good. Things are not always the way they look. There will be many that will try to tickle your ears, but this is how one falls into total darkness, by opening one's self up a little bit, a little bit to evil, a little bit to darkness until the darkness sweeps in and then draws you into the darkness itself. This must be different with you.

I ask you to pray for the holy father. I ask you to pray for the cardinals and the bishops and all priests. Let nothing shock you nor disturb your peace knowing full well that the gates of hell will not prevail. Try as it may, the gates of hell will not prevail against Mother Church and the splendor of truth that abides in her heart. Remember this, remember this word and be true to yourself and true to Mother Church. Be true and faithful to the Father and to the Son and to the Holy Spirit.

7/11/13

I am ever present, and I am always present. I have been with you before you were even in your mother's womb till this very moment. You actually were conceived in my mind, and through the cooperation of grace came into being. And I tell you now that I have loved you with an everlasting love. Oh, I have seen your past, I see you in the present, and I know the future that I have planned for you. It is a future filled with gifts of my love, reminders of my presence, grace along the journey, forgiveness and mercy and unconditional love. If you knew how much I love you, if you would even be able to get a real glimpse of the love that I have for you in my heart, you would weep, you would surely weep and cry. When you look at a newborn child and you're filled with awe, that's only a glimpse of what I feel when I look at each of you ... and you in particular.

You see, I have a purpose and a plan for every single person, and I work through everything in every situation in every set of circumstances. I'm always working in my way in your life and in the lives of those that you love. When I say I will never leave you nor forsake you, they're not empty words. I am the living word. My words are full of power. My word is spirit and life and I would have you know that you were created in my own likeness and image. And when I looked at you when you first came into your humanity, imagine this ... I was in awe. You were the desire of my heart. I carried you when you were so weak and when you were broken. I assuaged your wounds and tears. I mended your broken heart. I forgave the sins of the past and I love you into wholeness when you are broken. I have loved you with an everlasting love. Let that be a word to your heart and to your mind and to your spirit. Never loose hope. Never feel that you've been abandoned. Remember those words: I have loved you with an everlasting love. Again, I will never leave you nor forsake you.

I ask only that you seek me day in and day out. I ask that you would remember that you are created in my likeness and my image and every child within the womb from the beginning of time to this very moment in time I have called forth into being. I breathe life into each and every one of you and if I withheld my breath of life you would cease to exist, yet you fail day in and day out to realize the magnificent gift of life that I have given you. I ask you this day to remember and never forget that every life, every single life, has a purpose and a plan ... my plan, my likeness, my image. And woe to those who crush and destroy that life. They might try to crush and destroy God, the Creator, in that image but I tell you this sin calls out for justice. I ask you to stand and pray for all your brothers and sisters who do not know this truth. I ask you to stand in earnest prayer for all those who do not understand the fullness of the splendor of this truth. You see, I have a plan for you and through your faithful testimony of what a merciful God I am, through your testimony of my love for you, the love that has set you free, given you new life, the old has passed away and the new life is experiencing that peace and joy and love. Share that love with one another. I have created life. You are part of my mystical body and so I call you, I call you to minister to one another as I have ministered to each of you to love unconditionally, to forgive over and over and over again. Be a peace-giver. Be one who brings joy in the depth of sorrow or light in the middle of darkness to someone's life. Be my hands. Be my voice. Be my presence. Be my heart in the world that desperately needs my love.

8/1/13

I am always ready. I am ready to heal and bind up wounds. I'm ready to dispel the darkness with the light of my love. I'm ready to always break the bonds and chains that hold you bound as well as your loved ones. I'm always there when you are tired and weary, when you are broken emotionally and physically and spiritually, when you are filled with anxieties and fears and depression. I'm always there, but so often you turn to me late, often last if at all, and then you are in awe when you see the power of my work released into the situation at hand that has taken you to despair or to worry or fear or anxiety. When you think things will not get better, when you're alone and you are weary and burdened because the tasks at hand and the responsibilities are burdensome ... I'm there. I'm always there waiting for you to turn to me, waiting for you to call upon my name. You see, my love is always present. My heart is always beating for each of you. There's so many who do not know me, so many who do not call on me, so many who have left me, and still so many who do not even know that I exist because their eyes have been blinded and their ears stopped up and their hearts have grown cold.

I want you, I want you to take my heart, my love, my compassion, and yes, my power out into the world. I want you to go to everyone, not just the ones you think would like a prayer meeting, not just the ones you think who are all alone and it would give them fellowship to come to church or to be part of a prayer meeting. I want you to go out to everyone. I want you to go out to be fishers of men and women and young people and children, for I am God and the God of all. There's so much I want to give my people but so often, time and time again, you're afraid to venture out into the deep, you're afraid of being ridiculed or misunderstood and so rather than to reach out and draw others to me, you go to the people you are comfortable with, the people that you think would be interested in a deeper walk in the spirit but you see, even though my heart is rejoicing, I am still asking you to go out to those of the byways, those who are on the outside looking in, those who are forgotten, those who have been discarded, those who have no one to pray for them. These are the people that need to hear the truth. These are the people that need to experience love, my love, unconditional love.

And the more you learn to turn to me, to trust me with your situations, not only will your loved ones be healed and delivered, not only will your friends be set free, not only will the situations and circumstances in your lives change, but then you will grow in grace and wisdom and knowledge, and this is what the world needs. The world needs you to go out, not to a couple, not to a few, but to go out to everyone and freely give them the good news, not so much by your words, but by your deeds and your actions. My mother heard the word, received it, kept it in her heart, and then took it out. She went immediately to share the good news. She acted upon the word that was given her. So too it must be with you.

8/22/13

Do you realize that the greatest gift that you have received in your lives ... it isn't the material things that are very precious to you indeed, it isn't even all the things of the world that you have desired and through your hard work have received. The greatest gift that you have received is the gift that I have given to each one of you, the gift of faith, given freely so that each and every one of you could enter into eternal life. What gift, what gift indeed could compare to the gift that was given so freely out of love, the gift that cost me everything. The price I've paid for you to receive this gift of faith ... the cost was my very life and I did it for you and yet you fail to realize the magnificent gift that you have received.

Oh, when things get tough and when life is dragging you down or when obstacles appear insurmountable, when your business is suffering, when there's trouble brewing in marriages, when there's broken relationships, when you're suffering in health or your loved ones are, or when I call one of my children home ... oh, surely then you turn to me. You lift the desires of your heart, you lift to me the hearts that are broken. But when things are going good, when life is full of light and sunshine and joy, do you use that wonderful gift of faith to draw others out of the places I've taken you from?

When I call you home, what legacy would you leave behind? Think about it. What legacy would you leave behind you? I tell you this night this great gift of faith that I have given you, this faith that can move mountains, this faith that can bring forth the healing power of the living God, this faith that calls down the mercy of God, this faith that brings my people closer and closer to the truth, the splendor of all truth ... this faith must be used, must be exercised, must be given freely to others as I have given to you. You have not paid the price and yet you received the priceless gift. So I tell you to give this gift freely to others so that they too can be lifted out of the places, out of the circumstances, out of the situations, out of the heartaches. Give it to them, this priceless gift that cost me everything. And I freely did it for you.

9/19/13

Do you really understand ... understand the truth that all good things come from me or do you feel all good things come from you? You pride yourself on all of your accomplishments or do you recognize that it is through my goodness at work that allows you to accomplish the good that you do? For you see, apart from me you really can not bear fruit that will last. I want you to open your eyes and your ears and your heart to my love. I want you to begin to see my love, my care, my tenderness in all the different situations that you find yourself in, through all the different circumstances of your life.

I assure you there will be much that will come to try to steal your peace. There will be much upheaval that will come to fill you with anxiety and fear and doubt. Need I tell you again ... place your hope and your trust in me. You have nothing to fear. You see, I want to take away your anxiety and your fears. I want to give you wisdom and knowledge and understanding, and the grace to work situations in your life that you're going through according to my good pleasure. There would be much to come to rob you of peace, but I am the Prince of Peace. I not only want to give you peace but I want to give peace to the world. I want to bring peace where there is so much turmoil, where there is hatred and bigotry and bitterness and resentment. These are destructive to the individual soul. These are destructive in relationships. These things are destructive in every aspect of life.

  I want you to invest your time, I want you to invest your money, I want you to invest your skills and your talents in the kingdom of God so that I can give you back a hundredfold. What are you invested in my son? What are you invested in my daughter? Are you invested in the things of the world that are temporary or are you invested in the kingdom of God that will bring you eternity, that will have you where I am, that will give you the peace of knowing that you have chosen the better part? There is much I want to say, much I want to tell you, but this night know this … have ears that hear and a heart that receives so that you can take these words and allow them to sink deep into the deepest recesses of your mind and your body and your spirit, and then take these words out to everyone that I bring you in contact with. My word is spirit and truth. My word brings life. My word, I assure you, will overcome the culture of death.

  Trust in me. What is out of your control is never ever out of my control. Trust that I am always in the midst of working all things together for a greater good though you do not understand, and many times wonder, if I even hear your prayers. Let me assure you, I do. Let me assure you too that your greater good is a desire of my heart.

9/26/13

When many could be confused, when many could be in turmoil, when many suffer for lack of direction or guidance … it is because they have not turned to me. I say to you, you have chosen the better part indeed. I have seen your struggles. I have seen your woundedness, not only your woundedness, I have seen your heart, the heart that seeks me yet continues to stumble and fall through weakness. But you have turned to me and my heart rejoices. For you see, unless my people turn to me in their weakness, in their turmoil, in all the struggles of life … unless they turn to me they feel alone, abandoned. They loose hope. They go into deep depression. I say that my light will dispel the darkness in everyone's life if they come and seek my face. If they humble themselves before me, I will not only assuage their wounds but I will draw them close to my own heart, the heart that has loved so much and has been loved so little in return. You see, I see your wounds. I see the deep hurts in your heart. I see the tears that you have cried. I know the feelings of alienation and rejection. I know the feelings of feeling that you were on the outside looking in. I know your feelings of you couldn't quite make the mark that others expected you to make. And I tell you now I will heal those wounds in your heart, not a temporary healing but I will heal them completely so that you can seek and find restoration, renewal and empowerment through the power of my Holy Spirit at work in you.

I have not left you nor will I ever abandon not even one of those that I have called into being. Never doubt that I will never leave you nor forsake you. I will always stand by your side. I will always speak words of encouragement to your heart. I will always go before you and prepare the way. I will always give you wisdom and knowledge and discernment when you seek first my kingdom. And so you see it is I who have called you. It is I who have chosen you. It is I who have called you by name and called you here to this place at this time in your life for I am the one who heals and binds up wounds. I am He who works every single thing together for your greater good and I will give you new life. I will give you a new zeal in your heart and I will give you my peace that the world will never rob you of. So place your hope and your trust, not in the things of the world, but place your hope in me for I AM and I will give you everything so that you can be the person that I call you to be: child of the most high God.

10/3/13

I delight in your praise, for you see, I call my people together to come and worship me, to give praise and thanksgiving. I call my people together to sing songs and to love one another because in loving one another they are loving me.

The world is so broken. My mystical body is so fractured. I see all before me and I see brokenness and heartache, confusion and doubt, animosity, hate, intolerance. I see death all around by taking the gift of life and destroying it. No matter how many times my word speaks of the dignity of each and every person; all life I have given. I want to sanctify. I want to restore and heal and renew. I want to heal my broken body. I want all to be one in me. I want everyone to begin to have a deeper understanding that I love all. I love each and every one of my creations. I am the divine physician and I want to heal and bind up wounds. I want to wash away tears, heal broken hearts. Where so many are walking in darkness, I want to invite them deeper and deeper into the light of my love.

I want you to not only be a channel of my peace, not only to bring my word to others ... my word is spirit and life ... so I also want you to bring my life to others, the life that will convict, the life that will transform, the life that will bring peace, and the life that will bring clarity and understanding for all those who are so misinformed and for all those who do not know me. I am the way, truly there is no other way. I am the truth. No matter how many nice words will tickle your ears or the ears of others, I alone am the truth and I am indeed life. I want to resurrect all those, all and everyone of those who are on the way to destruction. Oh, that they would know me, that they would open their hearts, their minds to my saving grace. But you see, they do not hope in me. They do not trust in me. They do not believe in me and so I send my disciples ... these disciples in these days when there will be so much chaos. I send you out as light. I send you out to be the good news when there is going to be so much bad news in the world. For you see, my plan is a plan of salvation. My plan is to save all who hope, believe and trust in me.

So you see, I have not come just for you, I have come for your whole household. I have come for your neighborhoods, your parishes. I have come to save the world and its inhabitants from total destruction. Why? Because I can make all things new, because I am the healer of healers and the lord of lords, because I alone am the solution for every problem and the answer to every question. So stand firm in the truth. Let not your ears be tickled but know that I alone am the way and the truth and the life.

10/10/13

So many in the world today, all over the world, in every corner of the world, have closed their ears to the truth and have closed their heart to the moving of my Spirit. So many say there is no God, and others say God never answers prayers, and still others ask why do all the horrible things in the world happen if God is a loving God? And so, many have turned away. They have asked but have not received because they have asked wrongly. They have sought their will and not mine. You see, I'm a loving Father. I love my children and I know what is best for them. Many believe that I do not exist and if they look at the world and all the magnificent, picturesque beauties of my creation, how could they doubt? Many wonder ... is there a purpose and a plan for their life, for they do not feel joy or peace, and it is many who have all that they need financially, often many who have everything they need monetarily and materialistically. It is because they look to the world to fill the voids and the emptiness deep within them. They go after more things thinking they will be happy and nothing further from the truth could be. You see, if they seek my kingdom they will have all the things that they are really searching for. They'll have peace, they'll have joy that will give them strength and they will have light that will dispel the darkness ... my light, working in them and shining through them.

  They put up their own road blocks. They put on blinders because they do not want to see a suffering God. They do not want to believe in a crucified God. It is too hard for them to believe in suffering. They do not want a suffering servant. They do not want a suffering savior and so they try to sanitize the cross out of existence for this way it is easier to believe in themselves, easier to strive for what they want, and easier to reach the goals they have set. And yet at the end, they are empty ... broken ... because they have failed to recognize that I alone am the one that can fulfill their life. I alone am the one that can give a joy to them that the world can not take away nor give them. They fail to believe in me because they believe more in man. How vain. How foolish. How sad.

I am coming, make no mistake about it. And when I come, all those who belong to me, all those who have waited faithfully, all those who have placed their hope and their trust in me ... their hearts will rejoice. They will be filled with a peace that will overflow. They will be experiencing a joy that no words could express.

This is the message you must take out into the world. The kingdom of God is within you and it's only those who close their ears to the truth, put on blinders, and fill their hearts with the things of the world that can not experience it. So you must be the bearers of the good news. You must go out into the world, you who are faithful, sinners but faithful sinners, weak but strong in me. You must take this message of salvation to those who have ears but are not listening, those who's hearts have grown cold and those who's eyes have been veiled. Now is the time, now is the hour. Go out into the world and allow your light to shine brightly ... the light of Christ. Illuminate every area that you go into with the light of my love. Reach out to those who are suffering. Give to the poor and bring a message of God to those who know Him not. Bring a message of love, peace, mercy to the brokenhearted, for all those who are searching, they know they are empty and are missing the mark. I send you out that you might ignite a fire everywhere you go with the fire of my love that burns within you.

10/24/13

I'm calling you. I'm calling each of you by name. I want to speak to each of you. I want you to learn to be still and in the stillness your heart will be open to the powerful moving of my Spirit at work in you. You busy yourself with many things but you rarely take time to be still and to listen. This is what I call you to. This is what I want you to begin to discipline yourself ... to sit, to be still. I can accomplish so much in the quiet heart, in the still spirit, because your heart is open and you are vulnerable and you are listening ... and so I speak.

I am preparing my people. I am preparing each heart individually and collectively. I am pouring out my Spirit. I am healing wounds and breaking bondage. I am breathing new life and refreshing you, especially you, you who have grown weary, you who are tired, you who feel so burdened at times. I am pouring out my Spirit on all that are not only gathered here but all those that I am raising up to be my witnesses and I tell you that your fears, your anxieties ... they can be a stumbling block to becoming still, to allow the quiet light of my love to minister to you, to heal those things in your life that stifle the Spirit of God at work in you for I have a mighty work for you to do. I know your fears and your concerns for your family members, your children, your mates and your prospective mates. I know all things. And I say to you now, come and find a quiet place and let us sit and talk together. I will speak to you and you will speak to me and it will be a beautiful prayer time because prayer is two people interested in the other and sharing and baring hearts, dreams, hopes, fears. That's prayer, when two people listen, two people speak and care deeply ... care more about the other than the self. This is a great prayer.

Nobody will ever love you the way I love you. No one will ever be willing to lay down their life for you nor sacrifice for you, and so I wish you to learn from me for I am meek, and as you know, humble of heart. This is the message I want you to take out to the world, to be meek and humble of heart, to be aware that I can do great things in you and through you, but it is my power at work in you, working through you. I tell you now, do not be concerned, do not fret, do not worry about your future. I tell you to trust me, to trust me each day anew. I know the plans I have for you. You need only trust in my care for you, and not only you, but for your children, especially those who are away from me. I am working powerfully. I am moving powerfully in the hearts of my people. And for those who do not know me and for those who have turned their back on me, I tell you I am raising up bright lights to dispel the darkness. I am raising up a mighty force in the hearts of my believers who will stand fast, who will be filled with holy boldness, who will know without a doubt that I am moving in them and through them, and with me all things are possible.

My Church will suffer much but remember this, the gates of hell will never prevail against her. Stay close to the teachings of the Church, these teachings are infallible. When you are confused and when you doubt, listen to what the Church is saying. Be attuned to the teachings of the Church and come to know what your Church teaches so that you can combat error, you can combat untruth.

Yes indeed, I am coming, and when I come I tell you this, I shall fill every one who has stood firm in faith, who has stood firm in trust, with my glory. I am moving now to bring the Church of the East and the Church of the West together. I will have one mystical body. I will not be denied. This is the desire of my Father's heart. It shall come to pass. Pray for unity. Pray for unity. Pray for unity and you shall see and be in awe of what I will accomplish. My mother has placed her mantle over the Church and as she places her mantle over the Church, Mother Church will guide you and lead you. You have nothing to fear. Be of good cheer and trust in my word for it shall come to pass.

11/7/13 (1 of 2)

So many of my sons, so many of my daughters are not at peace. Through all the twists and turns of life, there has been unrest in their heart, in their mind, and in their spirit. And so too they fail to recognize that I am Lord over those situations. You see, I have a plan for each and every one of you. You would be amazed if you even had a glimpse of my plan. The very things that you fight against, the very things that you struggle with, the very things that tend to rob you of peace ... often times it's because you sought your will rather than my will. But just like a detour sign, when there's road blocks, through the detour you are brought back to the point of your destination. Your destination is eternal life. I have a plan for you. I want to fill your hearts with a peace and a joy that I suffered and died for, so that you could realize, truly experience, the power of my death and resurrection ... the power of new life that I have come to give you. Do you not yet know, have you not grasped this truth, that before every decision, to come to me and to bend your will by saying "not my will but thine be done." It would alleviate so much heartache. It would alleviate so much anxiety. It would alleviate the turmoil, time and time again, that you come against. Do you think for one minute that there's a problem that is bigger than me? Do you think there is a set of circumstances in your lives or the lives of your children, your mates, your family members, that I can not work together for a greater good? You must come to me. I want to take away your burden. I want to give you my peace. I want to fill you with grace.

    Do you think that I don't see you crying in the night? Do you think I do not see the times that you've fallen into sin and because of this you are devastated? I tell you truly that if you say my name in the midst of temptation, the devil will flee you. This is my word to you. My word is spirit and life, and in times of darkness, in times of sin, which is death itself, I will give you light for the way to dispel the darkness in your life. I will give you the grace and the courage and the strength to pick up your cross and to come follow me, for where I will lead you will be a path that will lead you to eternal life. Did I not tell you that I would go and prepare a place for you? This place awaits you. I paid the price. All you need do is live your life each day in me, with me, and through me. I have said it to you before, if you only knew how much I love you, you would weep and weep and weep. You can not fully grasp nor understand the debt I paid for each of your lives and the lives of those in your life. I paid the price in full. There's nothing owed on the account. I ask you to trust me.

Because you fell or failed today, do not think that you will fall again tomorrow or fail tomorrow. That is a lie that you would choose to believe over the truth that I have come to set you free. I have a plan for you. I have a purpose for your life. I want to heal your heart and comfort your soul. I want to bring order into your life and into your families. I want you to experience the peace and the grace. I want you to experience my love. I really do love you unconditionally, you know?

Will you trust me? Today is a new beginning. Moment to moment is a new moment. Will you trust me in the present moment? Will you allow me to be Lord over your life? I assure you my way is so much better and easier than your way for I alone am the way, the truth, and the life. Come and follow me along the way that I have chosen for you. Do not be concerned about those that you love. Do not be vexed over your children, your mates, your Country. Trust in me. Trust in my mercy. Trust in my love and be willing to go forth empowered by my Spirit to walk boldly into a new day, into a new moment, into a new hour to speak the truth that will set my people free.

11/7/13 (2 of 2)

The time is coming when dark shall be light and light shall be dark. North shall be south and south shall be north. But all of this is part of my plan so trust in my love, in my divine wisdom, and in my divine mercy. Do not let your heart be troubled or afraid. I say it again, be not afraid but receive power from on high. I did not leave you orphaned. I will never leave you nor forsake you but I say it again, light shall be dark, dark shall be light, north shall be south and south shall be north. Be not afraid.

12/5/13

It's all about my mercy and my love. It's all about the tenderness, the strength, the power, the might that I infuse in each one of you. It's about my love for mankind. Oh, how I wish that people would understand my great love and mercy. You have begun to understand. You have begun to step out in faith. You have begun to share even when it's been uncomfortable about my love and my mercy, my forgiveness and my power. So many who are hellbound need to hear that truth. You see, I want to break the chains that hold them bound. So many today are lost. So many are in situations that are drawing them deeper and deeper into darkness. So many are walking along the roads of perdition. I want them to know of my love. I want them to know that I have the power that where they've been dead in sin I will resurrect them in new life, that I have the power to infuse into everyone's life the light that dispels the darkness. You are so easily distracted. Oh, you know that I'm here. You certainly know and have come to understand my great love for you, but so often you keep that love, so often you keep my mercy in your own heart and in your own life. But see, I share my mercy with you so that you might share it with others. You see, I have forgiven you not only once, twice, thrice, but time and time and time again, and so I ask you to be patient with those that you must forgive. Do not think because you have forgiven them once that you're not called to forgive again. Many are lost and I've placed them in your life so they can be found through my love and my mercy and my grace. I have seen such tragedies take place because they have not turned to the God who has created them, who knows them better than they know themselves. They are incapacitated at times to move forward with their lives. They are broken, they are wounded, and yet they still do not turn to me, and so I say to you, open your mouth and speak of my great mercy and forgiveness and love. Open your eyes and look at those who are less fortunate than yourself and reach out to them, minister to them, care for them.

  I am waiting, I am waiting patiently, and I call all the day long but they still refuse to hear. They are lost but I will seek them out and I would not have you feeling that situations are hopeless. I would not have you feel that there's no way this person will turn their life around. Do you know who's hands you're entrusting them to … the very hands that created them, the very heart that has loved them with an everlasting love. Do not be foolish. Never ever give up. Though you might grow weary and tired and frustrated, never ever give up.

Many will push all your buttons. Many will push you to the edge to see if you will still love them because they feel they are unlovable. I tell you now, my love, my love alone will heal the wounds in their heart. My forgiveness, my mercy will break the chains that hold them bound. If you love them, the greatest thing you could do is to commend them into the heart that has loved them with an everlasting love, for you see, I will indeed set my people free. So you must come to understand, you must come to really believe that there's absolutely nothing impossible with me.

12/12/13

I'm asking you, I'm asking you from my heart to your heart to go out into the areas that you live in, work in, within your families and extended families … I want you to go out and be my presence to them. I want you to step out of your comfort zone. I want you to be filled with holy boldness that you have received when you were baptized and strengthened in Confirmation.

You see, you say you don't have what it takes. Oh, I've heard you say it on more than one occasion. You've said it to others, you've even said it to me: "Lord I don't have what it takes", but that's a lie. It comes from the father of lies. You see, you do have what it takes. It takes the power of my Spirit at work in you to give you courage to step out of your comfort zone. It takes the power of my Spirit filling you with holy boldness to speak words of edification, to speak words of truth that will set my people free, to speak a word of comfort, to speak a word of great expectation of the joy, the peace, the forgiveness and the mercy that's available to everyone.

You see, the difference between Judas and Peter ... you know they were equally loved ... and yet one turned and repented and cried out for forgiveness and mercy and received it, and one lost all hope and focused in on himself instead of turning for love and mercy and forgiveness. That's the difference and you see, there are many out there who look at themselves and feel they are not worthy, who feel that they have hurt too many people, broken too many hearts, fallen and fallen again time after time, and so they despise themselves and they buy the lie from hell that they can never change because they are a failure. They buy that lie from hell that they are no good and they're not loveable, but you see, you have the capacity through the Sanctifier to love the unlovable and to forgive what would seem to be the unforgivable. You have the capacity to love in my name, to love as I have loved you. This is all it takes: to love as I have loved you, to forgive as I have forgiven you.

Go out into all the different places of your lives whether it's your business, your home, your parish, your neighborhood, your Country. Your Country needs you. It has been enough to be silent. It has been enough to turn a deaf ear and a blind eye to what is going on in your Country, and so I need you to have eyes that see, ears that hear and a heart that will love in my name, that will speak the truth whether it's convenient or inconvenient, to be my healing balm in the world that is bruised and broken and bleeding. Tell them about my blood. Tell them about the blood I shed for everyone and tell them too that though they feel they are unlovable, I love them with an everlasting love. Tell those who feel they are not worthy that nobody is, but through my love and my mercy and my forgiveness, I have deemed them worthy to lay down my very life so that they might experience life to the full.

Go therefore and make disciples. Bring my people home, home to the one, holy, catholic and apostolic Church. See, your mission is her mission which was my mission.

12/19/13

You see, I have called you here. I have called each and every person here, and it was by grace and faith that you responded to the call, you just didn't one moment decide you're going. You see, grace was at work in your heart so you yielded to the prompting of my Spirit. And have I not told you … have I not told you that this is where I have called you so that you can bloom where you're planted? Have I not opened your eyes that you could begin to see me in others? Have I not opened your ears to hear new truths and to accept them readily into your own life and act upon them? Have I not touched your lips and filled you with my words so that you could speak of me with love and power, and have I not touched your hearts, the hearts that were once away from me, the hearts that grew weary and tired and were burdened, the hearts that were filled so often with sadness and emptiness, confusion and doubt? Have I not been faithful because I have taken those hearts and molded them and transformed them to reflect my own heart and the heart of my mother? You know, she really is the closest to my own heart. You see, because while I myself was being formed in secret, I rested beneath her heart until the perfect time to come into the world to save, to heal, to renew, to refresh, to strengthen. Have I not loved you tenderly? Have I not held you close to my own heart when you felt there was no one else who could love you, when you felt that you couldn't measure up to everybody else's expectations, when you felt you often times missed the mark, when you have felt abandoned, rejected, even lost? Have I not molded and transformed your hearts to be like mine? Have you not felt that new life of my Spirit, my gift to you? Have you not felt that grow deeper and deeper into your heart? Have I not called you here to renew you, to strengthen you, to teach you? Let your hearts be grateful, for many are called, but few are chosen.

(END OF VOLUME VI)

Volume 7

Nihil Obstat
Rev. Msgr. Joseph G. Prior

Imprimatur
Archbishop Charles J. Chaput
Archiepiscopus Philadelphiensis
October 18, 2018

No portion of this book may be reproduced in any form without written permission from the Publisher:
Morning Star – New Dawn Ministries
P.O. Box 1446
Blue Bell, PA 19422
If unavailable in local bookstores, additional copies of this book may be purchased by writing to the Publisher at the above address.

Copyright, 2019 By Kathleen McCarthy
ALL RIGHTS RESERVED   ISBN 978-0-9641873-3-7

Artwork by Margaret M. Matt

1/9/14

I hear so much of the moanings and groanings ... so much grumbling. I hear complaints and I see fear struck in the hearts of many of my people, and I speak to your heart this night. My perfect love will cast out all fear if you open your heart, your mind ... open it to me. You see, I am the light of the world. I am that light shining brightly as a safety, and I would have you call to me when you feel overwhelmed by darkness. For you see, you are children of the light. I want my light to shine so brightly through you. I want my light in you to dispel the darkness, and so I say: why do you fear, why do you tremble? Why are you anxious about many things? Have you not understood yet that my love conquered all ... that my obedience, even unto death, conquered all ... that my mercy, my power, my grace conquered all? I call you too to be conquerors. I call each of you.

When you feel that there's so much darkness in the world, and there certainly is, you must not focus on the darkness. You see, you are children of the light and the enemy's plan is to get you to focus on the darkness so that you will be distracted from the light. I am the light of the world. My light shining in you and through you can dispel all those fears. My light shining through you can draw your focus, your attention, back to the mission at hand, to go and make disciples.

I have given you the beautiful gift of faith. You have not earned it, it can not be earned, but I have given it freely to you that you might give it to others. I want you to allow your light to shine brightly. Yes, I want your lights to shine brightly. For you see, when you realize that you too are my light shining in the world, you will not easily be distracted. Your focus will remain on the mission. Your focus will remain on moving forward into new life and being bathed in the Spirit of my love to allow my light to go forth to those who are in total darkness, who are on the road to being lost. Do you see ... do you see the power of your mission? Do you see the call on each one of your lives? I do not call you for you alone. I call you for others so that they too might walk in the fullness of light and in truth filled with the Spirit, my Spirit, characterized by the very image and likeness of the One who created you ... my Father and your Father.

So do not complain. Do not grumble. Do not be distracted. Do not give up hope. Do not be depressed, and never fall into despair. Do not give the enemy his chance to work on you but think of me, my life in you, my light through you, my grace helping you grow into all that I call you to be. Be at peace and know that I have bathed you in the living waters of my love and of my Spirit.

So go, therefore, and make disciples. Go, therefore, and dispel the darkness. Go, therefore, as salt to bring out the best in everyone you meet, even your enemies.

2/6/14

A mother always carries that love in her heart for her children. She always remembers a child within her womb. And so too it is with every father that he remembers that child growing within his wife's womb. A gift, a gift of life entrusted into parent's hands.

But just as my Father loves each and every one of His children unconditionally, He continues to mold and discipline, continues to transform and enlighten and heal His children. And those that seem the farthest away, they don't recognize it that my Father is the closest to them because He weeps and morns for His children.

And so I ask that you would entrust all of your children into the heart of my mother, the mother who holds all of you in her heart. The mother who held me underneath her heart. So I call on you to remind you to lift your children to me through my mother. A mother never forgets her child and even if she did, even if she did, if it were possible, my Father will never forget you. He has loved you with an everlasting love and He loves your children with an everlasting love. He never forgets His own.

2/27/14

Have I not told you? Many times I have spoken to your heart. I've spoken to you through others. I've spoken to you mainly through my Holy word at Mass, spoken to each of your hearts as I come deeply and commune with you at Holy Communion. I say it again, those who wait upon the Lord, their strength will be renewed. I want you to ponder this thought.

There's so many that feel that they can't go on, so many that feel that their prayers are not being answered, so many who are broken and depressed and so many who are confused and so many who doubt, so many who just don't believe. But I tell you as one who knew you before you were even in your mother's womb, that I know everything. I see the big picture. I know exactly when to move in your life, when to move in the lives of others. You see, when you wait upon me, when you wait upon the Lord not only will your strength be renewed but you will be indeed in awe of the magnificence of my love. I want to sing a new song in your heart. I want to heal and comfort my people. I want them to look deep inside and see the ways that they need to surrender because when they surrender to me I do not leave an emptiness within them. When they give me their burden, when they give me the things they struggle with, when they give me their sinfulness, I will not leave a void but I will fill every part of your being with more ... more than you could hope for, more than you can expect, more of me and less of you. For you see, the desire of my heart is to not only renew your strength but to wash you and cleanse you, renew you and restore you in faith and hope and in love. For my desire is to give you that peace that will well up within you and truly dispel anxieties and fears and doubts and confusion.

And you see, I not only want to do this for you, I want to do this for those who you pray for, I want to do this with your loved ones, I want to do it for all those who cry out "Where are you Lord?" They have not learned yet that I am in their midst and I ask them to call to me and ask for help. They seek it in so many other places. They try to assuage their wounds and their scars and their hurts, but you see, I am the healer of healers. I am the Divine Physician. "I am" and so, therefore, I want to bring new life. I want to bring a deeper love, a deeper passion for the kingdom of God and so I ask you this night to surrender those things in your life that would stifle my Spirit at work in you. You can not do it you say? You can't do it for yourself and you can not do it for others unless I am in you and moving through you. It's not about you, it's about my power, my Spirit, at work in you reminding you of everything that I ever said, reminding you of all that I did so that you can begin to hear my voice, that you can begin to think with my mind, my thoughts ... that you can begin to walk empowered by my Spirit full of holy boldness to speak the truth, but to speak it always in gentleness.

This is the hour. This is the time that I am raising up my people to be aware of who I am in them. Repent indeed day in and day out so that I can fill you with power and grace.

3/13/14

I will send out a beacon of light. I will send out this beacon to draw others back home to my one, holy, catholic and apostolic Church, the Church I myself instituted. You see, I wait, I hunger and I thirst for souls. I wait patiently for those to come home, and you see it is through your love and your mercy, your forgiveness and your compassion that will change the world a heart at a time.

I ask you this very moment, I ask you to think of those you have not forgiven. I ask you this very moment to think of the person or persons in your lives that you have not been reconciled with and then I say to each of you, make a decision, act on the word you hear. Do not hear it and then go about your merry way but let this word seep deep into your heart and into your soul, and act on it. That's what faith is all about. I ask that you would remember that I am working in you and through you. I am transforming you. I am in you and molding you day in and day out, and as much freedom as you give me to work in you I will create in you a new warm, loving, merciful and compassionate heart. You see, this is what warms the coldest heart. This is what convicts the most violent sinner. This is what changes minds and hearts from hate and distain and unbelief to love, hope and mercy. Now is the time. Allow me to enter into you moment to moment, day by day, and allow me to transform you. Allow me to transfigure you to be more perfectly my likeness and my image in the world.

I send out a beacon of light, a beacon that will draw others who have wandered off, a beacon of light to draw others back to the truth. It is in place. It is time, and I call you not only to hear this word but to act on it. My people have no vision. My people wander aimlessly after "this" idea and "that" thought and they go into "this" church trying to find the truth and they continue to wander because it doesn't meet up with what they want. Every heart and every soul longs for the living God in His fullness, in His word and in the word that became flesh and dwells in every tabernacle all over the world ... not a part of me, but all of me. I will indeed send a beacon of light to touch minds and hearts to convict them in the spirit of my love, to reach out to those who do not know love and when you look at them with love, they will be renewed. When you look at them and reach out to them in mercy and compassion and love instead of judgment, they will see me in you. One heart at a time. One person at a time. This is what you were created to do. Yes, each of you were created to be my likeness and my image. Each of you are called to be Christ-givers. So ask me, what is it that you want me to do and then listen in the silence of your hearts and then act on it.

Now is a time of mercy. Now is a time I am raising up my people and sending them out to bring back my sons and my daughters to our one, holy, catholic and apostolic Church ... one universal church ... one shepherd ... one flock. Do not loose hope but allow my Spirit to move in you and through you for I am transforming you. I am moving in you and creating within you all of the things that I call you to act upon. I give you gifts of creativity. I give you gifts of wisdom and knowledge and discernment. I give you so many gifts. To one I give the gift of music ... to one, preaching ... to one, teaching ... to one, healing, and to some, all of these gifts. I will give these gifts in the measure that I know they will be received and used for the glory of God.

3/27/14

In the darkness and in the ensuing darkness, it is this time that people look and they fail to recognize the light. They fail to recognize that in me, the light of the world, they will find that the darkness can be dispelled. This is a time of urgency my people. This is a time for all those who have walked away and all those who do not know me. This is a time of tremendous grace and so I want you to understand that when I say this is a time of divine mercy there is an urgency in this message. There is an urgency in this time … now … today. I want you to have ears to hear my word.

You see, many do not even know, have not even yet begun to understand that they are living in darkness. They have become accustomed to the dark and that's why they don't want to come close to the light for fear that all of those deeds will come to the light. But what they don't realize is as they come and turn to me, the light of the world, that I will not only dispel the darkness but I will heal their broken hearts. I will heal their minds, their bodies, their spirit. I will take them out of the dark and draw them into the warmth and healing light of my love. Do not expect those who are away from me to find their way back to me without your help. Have I not said it time and time again, have you not heard it from generation to generation … you are my mystical body and so I put those in your path that I would have you speak to. Tell them of my great love, my great mercy. Invite them back, invite them back into the fold. Invite them back into our Church. Invite them back. They are hungry, they are thirsting for the living God and know it not. But see, you are the ones that can invite those to come back. It is you. I will place people in your life. They're all around you if you would only take the time to enter into the moment. I want you to speak. I want you to invite. I want you to communicate my love to my broken body. A time of urgency because of the need. That's why my mercy is flowing. That's why my mercy is going out so that when they hear their hearts will be moved.

I tell you now is a time, many do not see. They are in spiritual blindness and they've tried to fill the wounds of their hearts and their souls with things and people. I am the Healer of healers. I am the Lord of lords and the King of kings. I am the light, the light of the world. This light I have given to you through your baptism. I call you to be that light in the darkness. Go out to those who you would never expect to see in church. Go out to those with love and mercy and hospitality and invite them to come and see. That's all I want you to do. Invite them to come and see. I will open their eyes, their mind, their heart and their spirit, because in taking the invitation they will have ears to hear and a heart to receive.

So go forth. Be aware of the opportunities that I send into your lives when you least expect them. I am a God of surprises and I surprise in a moment. Be ready my people. Be ready to shine your light brightly, the light that dwells within you, the light of Christ, my light. Be ready to allow it to shine through you to dispel the darkness. I have overcome the darkness. I am all light and all love.

4/10/14

You are the new evangelization. You are the fire, the fire that ignites a flame in the hearts of others when you walk in the Spirit of my love. When you walk in the Spirit of my love, you automatically attract others. And when you speak my word, the word of love, the word of mercy, the word of compassion and healing and deliverance ... when you speak my word those who receive it will be drawn deeper and deeper into the living water that will wash away the debris, that will stir up the gifts that lie dormant within them. And although many will be offended by your words, many will hold their ears and will not want to hear though they have ears they will not want to hear, and though they have eyes, they will not see and their minds will be closed. And so I say to you, you are the good news. You are the new evangelization. And not only you but all those who are walking the way, who are walking in truth, who are filled with my life, who've allowed the Holy Spirit to well up within them dispelling anxiety and fear and doubt, continuing on the way, continuing to have their mind and their heart set on the cross before them, walking the way of love in spite of all those who jeer, of all those who make fun of, reject, all those who refuse the truth. You just keep walking in the way of love. You just keep talking and speaking my word. You just keep walking and reaching out to those in need. You keep reaching out so that I can assuage the wounds, the scars and the hurts that dwell in my people.

You see, the Spirit of the living God that dwells within you, the same Holy Spirit dwells within my other people but there is so much that has covered over their minds, and their hearts have grown cold and they have so much that their eyes are fixed on in the world, not on the cross before them but on the things of the world that they want, the things of the world that they seek out and search for and are willing to do whatever it takes to reach their goals regardless of how many people are wounded as they reach for those goals. So you see, you keep walking the walk. You keep talking the talk. You keep lining up with my word. You keep reaching out. Never give up. Never, ever give up. For you see, there are many that are just a word away. There are many who are close to turning to you. There are many who are hungering and thirsting. They do not know that I am the way, I am the truth and I am life, and so they harden their hearts, they close their mind and they turn away from the very truth that will set them free. And so I send you out into the vineyard. I send each of you out and as I send you out, I equipped you for every good work for I have given you the miraculous gift of the living God: the Holy Spirit dwelling within each of your hearts. And with the Spirit dwelling in you and welling up within you, you too as you speak, as you walk with your face to the cross and the wind at your back, many who would have been lost will be found for they would find me in you. So continue, continue to go forward. Continue to leave the past behind and do not worry about the future.

    You are so concerned about your children ... so concerned. Let me assure you this night, let me remove doubt and fear and anxiety from your hearts. Place your children in the heart of my mother. Place each of them, the youngest to the oldest, in the heart of my mother. Place your grandchildren there in the heart of my mother.

She will present them before the throne of God. She will safeguard those that have been given and entrusted to her care just as she did with me. My Father entrusted me into her heart, into her body. Did she not bring me full circle? Did she not bring me into the world to bring salvation to the world? Now she will bring the world to my Sacred Heart. Let not your hearts be concerned. I am working in your children's lives. They don't know it but you surely should. So do not fear and trust that I will give you the desires of your heart that not only you but your whole household will be saved.

5/8/14 (1 of 2)

    I say to you this night, I will touch your eyes that you will begin to see me more clearly. I will touch your ears that you will begin the journey to hear my voice and follow. This night I will touch your mind and enlighten your mind, your heart and your understanding of the beginning of the fullness of truth. I say to you in a very special way tonight, I will pour out my blessing upon you. You indeed came to see. Isn't this what I've told you in the scriptures: "Come and see". You have fallen in the hands of the living God. Come and see. Allow me to mold you, to transform you, to fill you with my unconditional love, then you might go forth and love others as I have loved you. I have a purpose and a plan for every life and the purpose and the plan originated in my heart, in my mind for you before you were even in your mother's womb. I have so much I want to speak to you about. I have so much I want to share with you. I have so much I want to give you and so I begin to take you on a journey, a journey into the very heart, the very sacred heart of my Son, Jesus. Indeed I have a plan for you. Come and follow me and I will anoint you, empower you and send you to bring this truth to others that they too might come on this journey, that they too might come and see.

5/8/14 (2 of 2)

When my word goes forth it never ever returns void. It indeed does the work it was sent to do. When my word is spoken it is not just spoken to one heart, it is not just spoken to one person. When my word goes forth it is meant to reach the hearts of others. For you see, it is only I, it is only I that can heal completely. It is only I that can forgive, renew, heal, make new. It is only I that can take you and your loved ones out of the darkness and bring all into my light, my glorious light.

People seek in things, peace. People seek in people joy, love, but you see, it is only I, others must come to me if they want the peace that will last forever. They must come to me if they want to be set free from the dominion of darkness. They must come to me and turn to me for I alone am God, for I alone can make all things new, for I alone can even raise the dead.

When I walked upon the earth they called me a miracle-worker and in the next breath they called me Beelzebub. The ones who know, the ones who receive my word are being drawn closer and closer to the fire of my love so that perfection is made perfect in their imperfect hearts. To those who called me Beelzebub and blasphemed the living God, theirs is a fiery end, a different fire, a fire that separates, a fire that burns. My word indeed is spirit and life. You can go nowhere else. There is no one who is the answer to all of life's mysteries, to all of life's problems … I alone am the one. And for all those who believe and follow me, for all those who know that I am the one and only true God, I shall empower and raise up to be my disciples, my apostles of this age, my light to dispel the darkness.

5/15/14   (1 of 2)

I would have you enter in, enter in to my love in a deeper way. I would have you enter in deeper and deeper into the living water, the water of my Spirit. I want to wash over you. I want to flow through you and I want to sprinkle all those that you come in contact with the living water of my Holy Spirit.

I want you to remember in a very special way each day, the spouse of the Holy Spirit is my own beloved mother. And I'll say to each of you, I'll speak this truth so that you will be better able to understand the importance of this truth: I've said in the scriptures that those who love their children, those who have cooperated with grace, cooperated with the living God to bring forth life, that I am aware that each one of you love your children, and I want you to think on this. Have the ears to hear but not only to hear but to act upon it and that is that my mother is concerned for all of her children. My mother knows that many of her children are in danger and so she intercedes constantly. You as parents with all your weaknesses, with all your faults ... don't you want to give your children the things that will keep them healthy, holy and safe? Again I say, don't you want to keep your children healthy, holy and safe? How much more my mother aches for her children who are wandering off. She constantly intercedes, but she wants you to intercede as well. You see, she places all the petitions that you pray for, she presents them to my own sacred heart through her immaculate heart and she presents them to my heart because I would not have one lost and yet many are on their way, many are on their way to being separated from me eternally by their own choice, by the choices they are making and have made. And so my mother weeps. She weeps for her children who have gone astray, for her children that have closed their eyes and will not look to see me. I tell you there are many on the road to perdition. There are many on their way ... yes, on the way to eternal separation. And so my mother comes time and time again. I send her more often than ever before and her message is urgent. She gives her children instructions just as you give your children instructions and you know how you feel when you know they are in danger. You know how you feel when you know they are making life choices that would set them on a road that will lead away from me. My heart is pierced once and for all and so my mother continues to come with an urgent message.

I say to you, will you not heed the message? Will you not heed the message to fast and to pray? Will you not heed the message to sacrifice for those who do not yet know the truth or those who have wandered away from the truth? This is indeed an urgent time. That's why I've sent my mother so many times and so often.

What do you not understand? I say it again this night, grace upon grace is offered. Will you be the instruments in my hand? Will you be my voice to bring the good news? Will you bring my love to those who believe they are unlovable? Will you bring the message of salvation? Will you fast? Will you pray? Will you sacrifice for your brothers and your sisters who are on their way to eternal separation? My mother pleads for all and distributes graces from all the ways that you offer her your sacrifices and she presents them to me and then I bless and heal, bind up wounds. So you and I together ... you and I together allowing me to live in you and through you ... this is the call. This is the call that is going out. I would not have one soul lost. I laid down my life. They need only repent and turn back to me. I will love them into wholeness as if they had never been away. Pray, fast, sacrifice.

5/15/14   (2 of 2)

Remember, when you bring my love bring it always in gentleness. Only I read hearts. Only I know what is in everyone's heart and so I say to you, you know not where they come from. You know not why they've made the choices they have, but I tell you, do not worry, do not fear about what others will think, how others will perceive you. Do not be full of pride, look more about how I perceive you. I who created you before you were even in your mother's womb; I who knit you in secret; I who have loved you with an everlasting love; I who have formed you with my own hands. I have breathed my breath within you to give you life. If I called that life back, you would be gone in an instant. So focus on what I think of you. Focus on my love for you and when you are tempted or afraid or confused or begin to doubt, command Satan in my name to go. Remind him that he has no power over you. Remember that … he has no power over you except what you allow him to have. My perfect love will cast out all fear. Be not afraid for I am with you and will never leave you nor forsake you. You are mine and I have loved you with an everlasting love.

5/22/14

I call you to live in the world but yet not be part of the world. I call you to indeed be my witnesses. I call you to be still and know that I am God, and then I infuse you with my life with the beautiful gift of Holy Communion so that you can go out into the world and be present and allow me to work in you and be present to others who do not know me. And so you see, I want to reach out through you. I want to speak out through you. I want you to know that I am always in you and working through you.

You must never rely on yourself. You see, it's always me. I am the cause of your hope. I am the cause of your joy. I alone am the solution for every problem. I alone am the answer for all the mystery. I know being in the world, it is difficult not to see all the ways that are filled with darkness. I know it's difficult to speak and feel that you will not be well received, or even yet, misunderstood. But you see, as you eat my body and drink my blood I remain in you. I fill you and nourish you and then I allow you to see through my eyes. I enlighten your mind and understanding to my truth and I fill you with holy boldness to go out into the world and to make a difference. You see, I am the light of the world and if you remain in me it does not matter the darkness that surrounds you for you will never walk in darkness if you remain in me. I am the source of all light. I am the light of the world and so there's no reason to fear; no reason to be filled with trepidation; no reason to stifle my Spirit at work in you because you are afraid of what I might ask of you; no reason to doubt; no reason to fear or be filled with anxiety and worry. I am the light of the world and when you live in me and allow me to sup in you then you bring my light to those who are in darkness. There are so many in darkness, but I will bless and anoint you. You see, you are so concerned with calling out to me and asking me time and time again for "this" petition and "that" petition, and rightly so for where else can you go? I am the answer. I am the savior. I am the redeemer. I am the liberator, but yet when you are preoccupied and consumed with fears and worry and doubt and confusion, these things are not in me or of me. And when they come upon you, when you find yourself or your loved ones in these situations and circumstances, take it as a warning that you are outside of my divine will and turn to me and ask me to fill you with my Holy Spirit. Ask me to infuse you, suffuse you, with my life, my body and my blood and then I will focus on all your situations and circumstances and all the things that you consider problems and I will be in the midst of working them all through. So you need not rely on yourself but only depend on me for I am the light of the world and if you remain in me you too will not stumble, you too will not fall, you too will walk in the light of my love because I will go before you and light your path so you will not stumble and fall.

So rest in me. Live in me. Seek me in all things from the tiniest to the largest, and my light in you will dispel your darkness. I am indeed the light that gives light to everything else. Trust me, love me, follow me and allow me to light your path.

6/5/14

What is it, what is it that troubles you this night? What is it that you would want me to heal, deliver, strengthen, give new life to? You see I already know what it is, but I pose the question to you this night that you might take stock of yourself and know, know that I wait, I wait to help you, to heal you, to deliver you. I'm always waiting. I will not impose myself upon you. I wait. I tell you now that I am the comforter; I am the counselor; I am the healer. I am the one that makes all things new. So look deep within your heart this night. What is it, what is it that is troubling you, weighing you down, confusing you? What is it that allows you to feel a deep sadness? What is it that robs you of peace? What is it that you depend on instead of depending on me? What is it that you focus on? What problems rob you of your peace? What circumstances do you allow the Spirit to be stifled in? Ask yourself, and then this night ... surrender ... surrender to me.

And once you surrender to me, I will show you a new way, once you offer me those difficulties, those problems, those anxieties, the fears, the doubts, the anger, the resentment, the loneliness, the bitterness, the broken relationship. Give it all to me, for you see I make all things new. I am the way. There is no other way to walk in peace and security and in hope and in joy. I am the way. I am the truth that will set you free, free to be able to surrender to me so I can give you new life, new life in my Spirit. I will counsel you. I will give you wisdom and knowledge and understanding of the things you would have no way of knowing or understanding. I will infuse your mind with new knowledge. I would soften your heart and tear down the walls that you have built up around your heart to protect yourself for you have been wounded many times. And as I take down those walls I will fill you with new life. I will fill you with joy where there is sadness. I have so much to give to you, but I wait. I wait for you to ask, and once you turn to me, once you surrender to me, those very things that weigh you down, I will lift you above them and I will give you great peace. I will give you a joy that you have not experienced in so long, a joy that is not of the world, a joy that will even take you through the deepest of sorrows, a joy that will fill you with confident assurance that I am always with you and I will never leave you nor forsake you though many of your friends have left you, forsaken you, gossiped about you, I will not leave you ever. I am with you always and I am molding you and transforming you day by day as you surrender to me.

    I have a plan. I have a plan for you. Do not think that I am finished with you for our life together is a new beginning day by day, a new conversion day by day, new light to dispel the darkness moment to moment. I am the only one who will never leave you nor forsake you. I am the truth and the only truth that can set you free. I am all love … unconditional love. Isn't that grand to know that you're loved completely and fully and unconditionally? Surrender day by day, moment by moment and let's live this new life in the Spirit so that you might live it to the full, so that you might be at peace and experience this wonderful gift of the Spirit day by day in your life. Lift it to me. Let it go and I will fill you with myself.

6/12/14

    Do you know how much I love each and every one of you? You really can not comprehend the fullness of my love. You love your children, but I actually formed them. I formed each of my children before their world began. I formed them in their mother's womb. I molded them and anointed them and breathed life into them. I have given my heart to each of my children to receive or neglect, and is this not so even with your own children at times. You give them your love. You take care of them. You nourish them. You put a roof over their heads and keep them warm. You take care of their needs physically, emotionally, spiritually, and you do the best that you can do, and you love them. And when they wander off you still love them, and then when they wound your heart and crush your spirit you want to throw up your hands and give up. They have ears, they do not hear, and they have eyes and they do not see the love that you have for them. How much more intense are the wounds of my heart when my children ignore me, when my children go their way and do not want me to go with them, when my children try to find things that fill what they feel are empty places in their heart and it takes them further away. Many times my children have done the unspeakable and the despicable, but you see I am a father that loves unconditionally and I continue to wait. I call each of you to continue to wait in joyful hope and in anticipation of your children coming back to me, coming back to you ... of your children realizing that they themselves have separated themselves. You have not separated them from your love. So continue to believe, continue to hope, continue to love, and the only way that you can do this is in me, but not only your children ... your mates, your siblings, your grandchildren, the people you work with, all family members and relations.

Oh, there are many that you can not tolerate. They continue to rub you the wrong way. They hurt, they ridicule and leave their scars on the inside. But I would have you remember when this takes place that they are striking out at the truth, that they are striking out against me in you. They are turning their backs on me in you but let it not be said that you were silenced. Let it not be said that you lost hope. Let it not be said that you despaired, for when you place your hope and your trust in me, then I will restore, heal, bind up wounds, bring together in the unity of my Holy Spirit families that have been separated, broken. Yes, place your hope and trust in me for I am a lover that loves unconditionally. I am a father who will never leave nor forsake those I created. I have sent my Son to redeem every soul, however, many refuse to receive it, and so your prayers are like incense. Never give up hope. Never give up on those that you care about even if they seem not to care about you. It is in me and through me and by my Spirit that you can do this. My Spirit will allow you the capacity to love the unlovable, to forgive the unforgivable. My Spirit within you will empower you to be a force to be reckoned with. You are my warriors and I equipped you well. Do not rely on yourself, your strength, your power, but rely on me for I who am in you are far greater than he who is in the world.

6/19/14

The Church is ever new. Just as the Church is ever ancient, so too I am in you ... ever ancient, the beginning and the end, ever new, always doing a new work in you and through you. As you step out into another new beginning in your life, as you step out into following the desire that I've placed in your heart as part of your livelihood, this is a new beginning for you, a new beginning in your life. It is I who have prompted and moved within you. You grow uncomfortable, you grow weary when you are not about my work, and so this is a new beginning. This is a new beginning in me and with me and through me.

You've asked me, is this what you want me to do, Lord? Is this what you want me to do with my life right now? And I say, be at peace and know that this is a prompting of my Spirit within you. It's a new beginning again, a new beginning ... exciting, but yet with much trepidation. Place all your cares on me. It is not for you to be concerned whether this new venture succeeds in your mind's eye. You see, it is about my purpose and my plan. I will bless it. I will bless this new endeavor ... so different from years of being comfortable in what you had always done. But just as assuredly, you will become just as comfortable in this new endeavor.

So I say to you, do not worry. Do not be concerned. Do not wonder how you're going to do it. Do not wonder what everyone else might say or do or think, but respond to my calling for you not to be idle for that's the Devil's playground ... an idle mind, a lethargic soul. And so I say to you, this is a new beginning.

Rejoice in it. I will bring you much joy. I will bless you, so do not worry and follow the prompting that I placed in your heart.

6/26/14 (1 of 2)

I am your hope. I am not only the cause of your hope but I am hope itself. When you place your hope in me in the midst of your trials and situations and circumstances and storms that affect you in life, I will give you a peace that will go beyond all understanding. You see, when you turn to me, when you hope not in people and places and things but when you hope in me, I will give you not only the right words to speak, I will give you the right path to walk on. I will give you the right decisions to make. I will give you all that you need for your station in life, and not only in you and for you but for those that you love, for those that you pray for, for those that you tend to, those that you care for. So place your hope in me and leave everything in my hands. Let your problems and your worries and your fears dissipate by placing all of them in my care.

My heart is the heart that has loved so greatly. My heart is the heart that continues to love unconditionally. My heart is the heart that was pierced for each of you and for all those who have been created. And so place your hope in me, the Resurrection. Place your hope in me, the Life, that brings life, new life, into all the areas of your life when you trust me, when you hope in me. For you see, when you surrender all to me ... your mates, your children, your grandchildren, your family members, your relatives, your business associates, your priests, your parish ... they are all in my heart. My heart is all loving and all consuming and when all is placed there you will no longer have a burden but the peace to know that once you have placed it in my hands, in my care, that all will work together for good. As you surrender, as you lift everything to me, and not give up, just give over to me, I will bless you and I will raise you above all those situations and circumstances, all the storms of your life, and it will be as if you were in the midst of the eye of the hurricane, at peace, at peace when all the fury goes on around you. That's what I do for mine who place their hope and their trust in me.

6/26/14   (2 of 2)

Come away with me to a quiet place my children. Come away with me. Tune out the noise of the world. Tune out the television. Tune out the radio. Tune out all that's going on in the world and come away to a quiet place with me where I can speak to your heart, where I can calm your spirit, where I can take away your fears and your anxieties. You see, I'm close to the brokenhearted, but you have to come away to a quiet place to allow me to speak to you, to allow me to embrace you, to allow me to pour the living water all over you washing away the debris, the noise, the turmoil.

Come away with me to a quiet place. A quiet place can be in the midst of a room of people. A quiet place can be in the midst of a busy day, that's when you focus on me, when you quiet your mind and your spirit and then it's you and I together, heart to heart, me looking at you and you looking at me in the spirit. You can find me when you're still. You can find me any time any place that you call to me and I will come to you.

7/10/14   (1 of 2)

I am doing something new, do you not yet perceive it? In the newness of it is my plan, my will, being accomplished. I tell you to wait upon me for to build with your thoughts, with your ideas is to build in vain. But to build taking on my mind, being filled with my Spirit, being transformed by the renewal of your mind is to accomplish something new in me, with me, and through me … this is the message that I give to you. Wait upon me. I have given you guidance and direction. Do you think I will not do it now or in the future? Have I not done it in the past? You see, your ways are not my ways, so wait upon me and I will guide you and lead you in this. My way is not your way.

7/10/14 (2 of 2)

You know, my people, that I am not something that people can look at and see. I'm not some object that people can hold and admire. I'm not something that people can draw other people into their homes to look at the display of my love or my power. What I do is show others my work in you then they can truly see, touch, and be immersed in my love through the sacraments so others can then see me living, moving, performing works of mercy and compassion and deliverance and healing, comfort, giving wisdom and knowledge and understanding, because I'm not a "thing", I'm a person … three persons in one. I'm the Father who created you. I am the Savior who redeemed you. I am the Spirit who empowers you.

And so I want you to know without a doubt that it is you, you bringing me out into the world. You see, I've chosen you. I've chosen you to bring the good news in the midst of so much bad news in the world. I've chosen you to do my bidding. I've chosen you to bring forth my will in the lives of all those that you come in contact with by you allowing me to work in you and through you by not stifling the Spirit. Remember who you are in me. Never ever forget that the living God dwells within you. Ponder this often. Yes, ponder this often. You do not have to try to run and find me nor does anyone else. You don't have to try to find a way to go up to reach me somehow because I came down to you because I loved you. I came to die that you might live. I was the light to dispel the darkness. I tell you truly that darkness and light will clash. The kingdoms of good and evil will clash and so I need you to be ever vigilant. I need you to remember that the triune God lives in you and works through you. Hard to comprehend ... yes, but the truth that will set you free to bring my truth to others.

You need not worry about situations and circumstances that come to pass. You need not be afraid for fear is not of me. You see, quite the opposite. I bring you to comfort. I bring you to reach out and comfort and give grace and strength through my power at work in you. So you must decrease and I must increase within you. Now is the time, a time to go therefore and make disciples and bear fruit that will last. Pass these truths on to your children and grandchildren, to your friends, to your family. Step out of your comfort zone and take the gift that you have been given and then give that gift freely to others. You have truly been given freely the gift of salvation. You have truly been given freely gifts of my Spirit. They were not given to you alone, they are given to give to others. Now is a time of mercy. Now is a time of grace. So go, go and do what you see me doing. Speak the words you hear me speaking. You need only look to the scriptures to know what it is. I have left you a show and tell, haven't I? I have left you my words. I have left you my Spirit. And so I tell you to open your mind, your eyes, your heart and your understanding for me to do the mighty works through you and in you. Go and make disciples.

7/24/14 (1 of 2)

I call you to fervently pray for my priests. I ask you to remember to pray for each of them every day. You see, your adversary, the devil, has come to attack, to plunder, to destroy the Church. He does not realize even today, because of his pride, that for every priest that he attacks I will raise up two in his place.

I want you to pray, pray for the Holy Father, my vicar on earth. You see, he's not just my vicar, just not the Pope, for you he truly is the vicar on earth for the universal Church. I would have you pray for unity in my mystical body and for this to come forth a new outpouring of my Spirit must be underpinned with your prayers. This is an urgent time. These are dark days, tumultuous days ... days that are filled and ravaged with darkness and anger, wars, famine, persecution. But you see, it is you the faithful, all your brothers and sisters remaining faithful even in the face of great peril ... sometimes even death. I want you to learn to see what faith means to those who are persecuted. They are willing to lay down their life rather than to deny my life, my name, my presence. And their faithfulness and their obedience and their love for me ... they are paying a great price throughout the world. But you, you know that the seeds of faith that will be planted in their place, that many will rise up. Many will be embolden to speak the truth. Many will be filled with my love and my mercy, my grace and my strength, and they will go forth and they will proclaim to the world the truth that Jesus alone is the only Savior of the world. They will go and proclaim this truth by which all men can be saved that believe in Him, my Son.

Will you fast? Will you pray for more priests? Will you pray for all those who are weary and tired, all those who are under attack? For you see, the adversary's plan is to attack the priests so that the Church would fall. But I remind you again of this one holy truth: the gates of hell will never ever prevail against the Church that I instituted. It is the one true Church and through the power and unity of my Holy Spirit I will draw others in to the fullness of truth. Other members that have been separated I will bring home. Others members that have not experienced the fullness of truth, I will enlighten their minds and their hearts through my faithful ones to come home to receive the fullness of truth so that they too can go forth and proclaim this message that I alone am the way, the truth, and the life. And that by my Spirit alone, by the Holy Spirit working in you and through you, many more priests will be raised up filled with holy boldness. But your prayers must underpin these vocations. What moral voice would be left in the world without the priests? How would you be fed and nourished on my body and my blood without the priests? How would you hear the words, "I absolve you from your sins?" How would you know that you are truly forgiven unless you hear my words through the priests in absolution?

Fast, pray for more vocations. I entrust this to you. You are close to my own sacred heart. And again I say as you fast, as you pray, as you remain faithful to your one, holy, catholic and apostolic Church, I will pour out my Spirit drawing others back to the truth that they left, pouring out my Spirit on those who have rejected the truth, and pouring out my Spirit on all those who have never known the truth. What a reward.

You see, I am outside of time and space. It is only "now." "Now" I ask you to remain faithful and to build up the kingdom of God by praying for vocations.

7/24/14   (2 of 2)

Honor your father and your mother. I tell you honor your father and your mother. Listen to my Son and then do whatever He tells you.

8/21/14

You see, I speak to you through my Holy word, I speak to you through my presence in one another, I tell you in little ways day in and day out and sometimes I shout through circumstances and situations so that you might hear and receive my word.

You see, I wish that you would come to me when your burden begins. You wait so long and you are filled with anxiety and fear, trepidation, even doubt sets in wondering if I'm even hearing your prayer. And you see, the desire of my heart is to bless you. The desire of my heart is to set you apart, to grow in holiness, to set you apart so that you can be a light shining brightly, not hidden. If you only knew that all you need do is call to me and I will come to you. You wait, you get frustrated, you even get angry. The different situations that you find yourself in … if you would only trust me. If you would only trust me to know that if I loved you enough to die for you, will I not work this through to your great good. I have waited time and time again for you to come to me before you get tied in knots. I've even offered you my mother as the un-doer of knots and yet you fail to ask her to untangle the mess that you find yourself in, and so you are filled with anxiety and fear and frustration. If you would just wait upon me you will be renewed in courage, in grace and strength and your peace would not be disturbed knowing that your deliverance is at hand. So why do you wait?

You wait because you trust more in yourself than you do in me. You trust more in your wisdom than mine. You trust more in your power to change situations instead of allowing me to transform you in difficult situations to see my power at work. If you only knew how much I loved you, you would weep and weep and weep. I love you. I have loved you from the time you were conceived in my mind and in my heart before you even came into the world, before you were even in your mother's womb.

These words are not only for you. These words will go out to the four corners of the earth, for my word will not return void. My word will do the work it is sent to do. I will heal families, reconcile marriages, heal bodies, minds, spirits. I will deliver from darkness and bring those who are on the road to perdition into the light of my love. I will bring them into my kingdom. I tell you this, make no mistake, as you trust in me and in my word, as you move to bring my word to others, I will do a mighty work. Do you believe, do you really relieve that by taking my word and bringing it to others it will surely go to the four corners of the earth? Why? Because I trust you. Imagine that! I trust you even though you fail to trust me. I tell you this tonight because there is an urgency. My light will indeed dispel the darkness. My love will overcome hatred. My peace will overcome fear.

I am about healing the family. I am about restoring the family. All families in heaven and on earth have taken their name from me. It is within the family that a mighty work will be done to renew the face of the earth. Take these words and share them with others for they are a light in the darkness. Take my mother and her motherly love for each and every one of you who's heart is on fire for love of you. Call upon her. Ask her to undo the knots that cause so much chaos in your life. I have given my mother to you to help you. I have given my mother to you as an example of faith, hope and love. Go and do likewise.

9/4/14

Do you know how often you've come to me, not once or twice or three times, but many, many times, often times asking forgiveness for the very same things, and I see your heart and I forgive over and over and over again. I see the desire of your heart. I see that you want to change. I see that you want to overcome the weaknesses and the areas in your life where you continue to fall. I see that you want something more. I see that you need my forgiveness. I see your heart that is repentant … the heart that sometimes doesn't even think about the fact that you come time and time again asking forgiveness and expecting it unequivocally, and you always receive it. Yet you are so slow to forgive others. You are so slow to offer your pardon. You judge harshly. You cut people off because they have hurt you or wounded your heart. And yet how many times have you wounded my heart? How many times have you cast me aside? Oh, maybe not meaningfully, but just assuredly you have. How many times have your actions been contrary to my will? My point is simply this: I want you to forgive as I have forgiven you. I don't want you to alienate. I don't want you to wound deeper the wounds that are in other's hearts that cause them to make bad decisions. I don't want you to wound deeper those who have chosen a different way. I don't want you to continually rip them down or tear them apart. I don't want you to alienate them and reject them.

    You see, I've shown you that I want to love you into wholeness. I always want to restore our relationship. I always want to bring you closer. I always want to repair and heal the wounds that sin separates us from, not from my love but from having that beautiful deep union. You see, that's what forgiveness is about. As I have forgiven you, so therefore I call you to forgive one another. When you refuse to forgive, when you reject, when you alienate, when you cut off, when you judge harshly, when you gossip, when your words rip down rather than build up … this not only wounds the heart even deeper of the person that has caused you grief, annoyance, frustration or pain, but you see it wounds your heart. It deepens the wound in your heart because you begin to feel angry, bitter. You begin to be upset and you know not from whence this anger and resentment and bitterness comes from. It's from the wound in your heart when you refuse to forgive, when you refuse to reach out. And you say you have given enough, you have forgiven enough … where would you be if they were my words to you?

    You see, I have come that you might have life and have it abundantly. I have come to give you joy in the place of your sorrows. I have come to give you peace where there's so much turmoil in your life. And you come and you praise me and thank me and your heart is healed and your spirit is free and you're full of love again. That's how these people will be when you forgive. I'm about healing and reconciliation remember, not only between you and me but between those that you've alienated because of the way they have treated you. And so I ask you to love, to forgive, and never give up by praying for those souls who cause so many of their own wounds and pain, and you are the healing love when you bring me to them in forgiveness, in healing, in love, in mercy and compassion. Let these words take root in your heart, in your mind and in your spirit. For you see, as I have loved you, so too I call you to love others.

9/18/14

I want to bless each and every one of you. I want to draw you close to my sacred heart through the heart of my mother. I want to speak to the deepest recesses of your heart. I want to bless you from your head right down to your toes, not only you, but all those that you love, all those of your household, of your family. Often times you have no idea throughout the day how I wait for you to acknowledge a blessing, a whisper of a word to your heart, an embrace in the spirit filling you with light, my light, when you receive Holy Communion with a pure heart. You see, I always want to bless you, heal you, renew you, strengthen you.

You who when you have a very important event coming up ... a wedding, a graduation, a retirement party, an ordination, a dinner party, an engagement party, all these wonderful things that bring you so much joy, you go out and you find the right dress and the right shoes. You pick out the right shirt and the right tie. You want to look your best. You want to feel good about yourself and so you go to great length to prepare yourself for your engagement, your party, your event, and rightly so. However, the greatest event takes place at every Mass all over the world. I'm truly present. I'm closer to you than you could even possibly imagine. This is a great event. History is being made. You and I together ... physically, spiritually, emotionally ... you and I together. I want to renew you and refresh you and strengthen you. I want to wash away the debris that makes you feel less than you are. I want to break down the barriers that you put around your heart. I want to remove the chains that hold you bound. Again, not only for you but for your whole household, for all those that you love.

And yet you fail to take full advantage of this spectacular event ... barely noticed when it takes place. You ponder me for a moment and then your mind wanders off. By the time you leave church you've left me behind. Oh, you love me. You want to live out that love but you don't stay centered on my presence within you. God coming to you ... the biggest event that you could have in your life. What do you do to prepare for this event? Has your soul and your heart been washed and cleansed through the sacrament of love? Think about it. Think about all the ways that you prepare yourself for others, for others to see you, and then think about how you prepare yourself for me, and do you wonder how I see you? I just wanted to share with you this night that you might be evermore aware of the magnificent gift that you have taking place on every altar all over the world when Mass is celebrated. Listen, listen to me speak in the silence of your heart when you receive me. Ponder this magnificent happening, this amazing event ... the God who created you, renewing you, strengthening you, healing you ... ponder it and focus on me. I will focus on everything else for you but commend your days to me, for when you walk in me and allow me to work through you, more than you could ever possibly imagine can be accomplished for my greater glory.

10/9/14

In many families there is division. In many families there are broken relationships. In many families there are those who have gone astray. Many families don't even talk to one another. You're my family ... children of the living God. My heart weeps because my mystical body is broken and not united and so I continue to bring unity into my body through the outpouring and renewal of my Holy Spirit. I said I would never leave you orphaned and I have not. I am working in you and through you in all of my children to bring unity so that there would be one shepherd and one fold. It must begin in your families. You see, it is within your power, through my power at work in you, to be reconciled to one another. You have no idea, no idea at all, when one would be called and one would be left home. You have no idea, no idea at all, of how I long for my people to be of one mind, one heart and one spirit. And so I say again it must begin with you. Be reconciled to one another. Do not go in anger when you leave someone that you disagree with. Do not stay angry at your children, your mate, people you work with, people that you live with. Do not allow the sun to go down on your anger, but go, forgive as I have forgiven you and be forgiven as I have forgiven you.

I have left you love letters from my heart to your heart: my word, my living word. They are my love letters to you because I love you enough, I thought you so valuable. I thought you were so beautiful that I laid down my life for you. Even in the midst of your sinfulness I love you. I want to love each and every one of you in such a way that you will begin to love one another as I have loved you. I say it this night again, reach out, tell those that you've been estranged from, tell those who are arguing and fighting and at odds with one another that this is not my way. My way and my path is one of love and mercy and compassion. You write a letter. You write a letter in my name through your name. Never give up on those who have wandered off, those who have rejected me or you or alienated themselves from your family. You see, these are the ones that I hold close to my heart.

I ask you to be my hands and my feet and my voice and reach out in my love, my mercy and my compassion to them. They are waiting. They don't know it, but they are waiting to be loved and accepted even in the midst of their failures, even in the midst of their brokenness, even in the midst of their sinfulness. Speak of my love, my mercy and my forgiveness. This is the healing salve. This is the song that must be sung, a song of joy, an ode of joy for my word brings life, joy, peace and grace and life.

Come against death and destruction and anger and bitterness and resentment. Come against these things with love, with mercy and grace. As I have forgiven you I ask, have you forgiven others as I have forgiven you? Now is the time. Now is a time of mercy. Now is a time of justice. Go out into the world and bring my mercy. Be a "reconciler" in my name. Do not count the cost.

10/30/14

I call to you. I call to you throughout the day. From my own lips I drop my word into your mind, into your heart, into your spirit. You came this night because I called you. I provided the way. I set this night apart just for you. Many times you hear others praising me for the ways that I have worked in their lives or in the lives of their loved ones or in the lives of those that they have been praying for and often times you question: why do I not hear your voice, why do I not have my prayers answered, why do you speak to others but I do not hear you, why do you move so powerfully in others but yet do not move in me? Yes, you. You know I'm speaking to your heart, to your spirit, to your mind.

Are you willing to surrender to me? I have told you time and time again that my ways are not your ways. If you could see with my eyes and my mind and my heart, you would be on your knees morning, noon and night praying for the way I am answering your prayers. But you do not see, you do not hear, and your heart does not sense that I am in the midst of working in and through your prayer intentions. You see, I have captured every tear you have ever cried. I have held those that you have loved and lost close to my own sacred heart. I want to assuage your heart, comfort your soul, give you grace for the present. Are you willing to surrender your time, trusting in my timing? Are you willing to surrender your livelihood so that I can move in you and through you to do all the things that I've called you to do? Are you willing to bow humbly before me acknowledging the fact that I will guide you and lead you and direct you? Humble yourself before me to begin to understand that as much as you love your children, your mates, your family, your friends ... I love them ever so much more. They were created in my likeness and in my image. They were created from my heart, my mind. Oh yes, I love them more than you could ever possibly imagine.

But some things are a mystery, some things you can not wrap your mind around. Some things you see, you can not understand. My mind is infinite, yours is not. my ways are so far above your ways because I see all, I know all and I love all, and so I'm constantly, not only moving in you and through you, but I'm changing circumstances. I'm moving in people's lives in ways that you can not fathom because it is not the way you expect that a loving God would work.

Poor you. My poor people. Do you not yet trust in the infinite ways of the God who created you? Have you not yet been able to surrender to my will to allow me to be the king in your heart, not you? You see, I love you more than human words can express. I love your families, your children. I love your enemies. I would not want one soul lost. And the things that you do not understand, the things that you say could not be from a God who is a loving, merciful, compassionate God ... remember your mind is not infinite. Your power is very limited. Your wisdom when not from above isn't perfect.

So begin to surrender to me a little more each day. I have placed you right where you can grow. I have placed you where you can grow in the power of my Spirit. Do you think it was your doing? Do you really think the things that you have accomplished were of your own accord, through your own power, your own strength, your own wisdom and your own knowledge? No. You see, when I bless you, when I anoint you, when I raise you up, when I work through you, it is a blessing and an anointing from the Spirit of the living God, make no mistake about it. Yes, you must use the gifts that have been given to you, but also know they are gifts from me to build up the body of Christ.

11/6/14

My light shall rise to dispel the darkness, the darkness in your lives, the darkness in the world. My light will shine brightly. The darkness has no power, no power whatsoever over you. You see, I came to deliver my people out of darkness and into my glorious light, and not only that, but that I abide in you. I live in you and work through you and because of this my light shines brightly through you. I call you to remember this truth: that no one or no thing will snatch out of my hand those that were given to me.

And so I send you out to bring them grace and peace and courage and strength, in particularly, to bring them hope when they've lost hope, to bring them joy, to bring the good news of the gospel to them because they have lost the joy of their salvation. I call you too to bring the peace that they have allowed the world to rob them of. We are co-workers you and I, and so I send you out, I send you out to bring my light into the world to dispel the darkness.

I have given you gifts, talents, skills. I have given you many, many gifts of the Spirit that come from above. If you do not use the gifts that I give you they will not only grow dormant but they will cease to exist in you. If you will not use what I have given you, you truly will loose it and I will give it to someone who will receive, knowing it is my work, my gifts, my grace, and therefore, use it freely for the up-building of the kingdom. Did I not say that you are the light of the world because my light shines through you? Ponder the fact. Do you really believe that I dwell within you? Do you really believe that my light is all powerful and that my light alone will dispel the darkness?

I will change you from being "victim". I shall give you the new name of "victorious". I tell you my all loving heart, my all loving Spirit, my all loving mercy consumes like a burning fire all those things that stifle the work within you that I have begun, but I will bring it to completion in you and through you if you turn to me. Turn away from those things that you know rob you of peace, that stifle my Spirit at work, and bring darkness and confusion and doubt. Ponder the thought indeed. You will find this to be the truth and this truth will set you free ... for I am the way, the truth, and the life.

12/4/14

You hear me speak to you through my word, and as my word is broken open you are washed clean by that word, the word that is spirit and life, my word. And through the power of my Spirit, through the power of my Holy word, my Spirit brings all things to fruition. In times of turmoil I bring peace. In times of anxiety and fear is when I bring you my constant breath of my Spirit to dwell within you and well up within you dispelling your anxiety and your fears and your doubts.

Indeed, I have told you to wait. I have told you to be alert. I've told you to watch. I tell you to be alert because the enemy is indeed looking to fill you with all the things that would stifle your peace at this time. The enemy comes to rob and destroy. I come to give life and have you live it to the full, and so I tell you to be alert. Do not let your hearts be so troubled. Do not be so thin-skinned that your feelings and emotions are hurt and wounded so easily. You see, these are tools of the enemy. This is a time of peace. This is a time that you should feel the joy of my Spirit within you, the joy that reveals the power and majesty and love of my Father for each and every one of you and for all of my people. I tell you to be alert where the enemy would be sowing discord at this time of preparation, at this time of anticipating my coming again. Where he would sow discord you need only turn to me for unity and peace. So be alert. Be alert that the enemy does indeed come to try to reek havoc in your lives, rob you of peace and the joy that comes from allowing me to be Lord over your life and to abide within you, deep within you, where your peace will not be disturbed. I tell you to watch, by "watching" means simply to keep your eyes focused on me. Fix your mind and heart and your spirit on me. I continue to come and I will come again. And so I ask that you not look to the things of the world and the worries of the world and all that's going on in the world, all the darkness, all the trouble ... it's all brought about by man's greed, man's selfishness, man's pride.

But you, I raise you above it, so I tell you simply "watch". Watch me. Hear my word. Follow in my footsteps. Do what you saw me doing in my word. Speak what you hear me speaking through my word. Wait, wait upon the Lord. You have heard it said, and it simply means wait for me to go before you and prepare the way. Oh, I have so much in store for you. I've placed thoughts in your mind, in your heart and in your spirit and they have truly come from me, and I've drawn you together so that you can be part of my plan. I ask you to wait on me. I ask you to wait until I bring those into your contact to speak of me, to rejoice in the presence of my life within your life. Without a word, without even a word, people will see by the way you're living that I am a God of the living and not of the dead. So I say to you wait, watch, and be ever alert. Where there's discord I call you to sow peace. Where there's anger and resentment and bitterness, I ask you to bring the breath and life of my Spirit into those situations. I ask you to be alert in the midst of the storm, for you to bring peace, my peace that the world and its darkness, and the storms of life can not rob you of.

Be aware of your brothers and sisters who are in need, who are lonely, sick, suffering, feel abandoned and rejected, and often times, so alone. These are opportunities for you to be my hands, my feet, and my voice. I have blessed you with much and I call you to bless others and to give the gifts I have given to you, and then the morning star will rise up within you filling you with a joy that is beyond all understanding blessing your home with a peace that nothing can rob it of. This is my plan, to bring peace and good will. I am your hope. Place your trust in me.

12/11/14

Have I not told you to count all of your trials, your tribulations, all the sufferings ... have I not told you to count it all as joy? Joy because with every cross I send into your lives, I send the amount of grace that is needed to carry it. And you see why people are dumbfounded. People are amazed just as they were when I walked upon the earth and healed and renewed and delivered. The people were amazed! And so too it is in these times that people will be amazed that in the midst of difficulties and trials and sufferings they will see a peace that will emanate from you that gives them hope, that gives them the time to ponder this. Surely, surely there must be a God or this person would be crumbled under such weight, but instead of being crumbled they rejoice. They find joy, and others are amazed, and they begin to hunger and thirst, they begin to long for that peace, that joy in the midst of sorrow, that light that dispels the darkness.

You must be "heralds" of the good news. You must be "heralds" out in the world so others can hear how God saves, edifies, heals, binds up wounds, delivers, makes all things new, gives hope to those who have no hope, gives joy to those even in the deepest of sorrow. You're called to be "Christ-givers". You're called to be my voice preparing the way, for I am coming, and so I call you to be my "heralds". I call you to reach out and proclaim the Gospel, the good news, that I am Lord, Savior, Prince of peace, mighty King, wonderful Counselor. "I AM", and because I am they have no need if they would only place their hope, their trust in me.

So you see, when they see you in the midst of all the inconveniences, in the midst of trials and temptations, in the midst of criticism and rebuke, alienation and even rejection, and they see the joy within you, they will be amazed and it will lead them to ponder and long that they too might come to know the Savior sent from the Father into the world to bring all the Father's children back home. This is quite a charge and you've been charged with it whether it's convenient or inconvenient. Will you take the charge and will you be my "heralds"?

12/18/14

This is indeed a time of great darkness. It's a time of turmoil, aggression. It's a time of being confounded and confused. It is a time when so many in the world today, my own creatures, those that I created with my own hands and formed them in their mother's wombs, those who have not lived according to the Spirit, those who have denied me, those who have walked away from me … yes, many even in your own households … it is this aggression, it is this confusion, it is this darkness that's in the world that they live in, that they abide in ... many do not know how to come out of it. They are stuck in the mire, they're incapacitated, and instead of falling humbly on their knees and calling for me to bring them into the light, they stay in darkness and choose the darkness over the light. And so it continues: more aggression, more evil, more chaos, more confusion, more doubt, more fear, more anxiety. For you see, these things are not of me, they're part of the dark. But I have come to dispel the darkness. I have come to deliver my people from darkness into the light, the light of my love, the power of my love, the healing balm of my love. They are so lost, so confused, and so broken. I continue to call to them, but they have ears and they do not hear. They have eyes and they do not see me, and so I send others out and I bring good news to those who are in darkness. I bring peace where there's turmoil and aggression. I bring clarity of mind where there's confusion and doubt. I bring the truth that will set my people free.

I tell you now, make no mistake about it, this a time of great urgency, great urgency! There's no time to waste. Don't just talk about what needs to be done. Just don't talk about what you should do, there's no time for this. It's a time of action. It's a time to go forth in the power and fullness of my Holy Spirit for it is only my Spirit at work in you that can change the hearts of others. I have come, I have come to be Lord and Savior, but the salvation cannot be received without those opening their heart to receive this gift, this gift of eternal life, this gift of peace, this gift of love ... unconditional love. This gift must be received. I will not force it upon anyone. The decision is theirs: eternal life or eternal death, eternal light or eternal darkness. Everyone will choose. I ask you, I ask you now to come to the understanding that this is an urgent time, an urgent time to go out and be light where there's darkness, peace where there's aggression, mercy where there's hatred and resentment and bitterness.

    I came to do the will of the Father, even to the shedding of my own blood. I only ask that you come and do my bidding everywhere and every place and to everyone I send you to or bring others to you. There is no need to preach and be hard-hearted over it or to look down your nose at others. Your faith alone is a gift from me as well. You had the wisdom to receive it, and so by grace through faith you were saved, and now I ask that by my grace in you, that by the faith that was given to you as pure gift, that you go and do the Father's will as well through the power of my Spirit that can do more than you could even possibly imagine. Look not to the times, it is for a time such as this that you were born, but look to me and continue to walk in the light, for the deceiver is roaming trying to steal and rob and destroy. So you must go and bring the light, my light. You must go in the power of my Spirit. It is only through my Spirit that lives can be renewed, people will be healed, strengthened, filled with grace ... and then they too will be sent out. Remember, it is a time such as this that you were born. You were born for a time such as this. There is no need to fear, no need to be anxious. Rejoice, rejoice that you will bring a message of liberation and freedom. I alone am the resurrection and the life.

(END OF VOLUME VII)